Busy Kids®

Busy Days
Spring & Summer

Table of Contents

©2002 by THE EDUCATION CENTER, INC.
All rights reserved.
ISBN #1-56234-519-2

D1473186

Manufactured in the United States
10 9 8 7 6 5 4 3 2 1

About This Book

Once featured as the popular Busy Kids® series, the contents of these eight great books have been restructured into two new books that make planning your theme-based units even easier! *Busy Kids Busy Days—Fall & Winter* and *Busy Kids Busy Days—Spring & Summer* will help you present complete theme units that feature the curriculum you need to fill your busy kids' days. Each theme unit is divided into several two-page sections featuring ideas for the following learning categories.

ABCs & 123s: Provide your little ones with the building blocks for school success with the ideas featured on the ABCs & 123s pages. You'll find fun and creative ideas for teaching basic concepts and building basic skills, such as letters, numbers, colors, shapes, counting, graphing, patterning, and much more!

Centers: These useful Centers pages present ideas for enhancing traditional centers and for creating easy-to-set-up thematic centers. Each idea reinforces skills while providing fun learning opportunities for children with different learning styles.

Circle Time: In the Circle Time section, you'll find helpful strategies and creative activities for one of the most essential segments of the preschool or kindergarten child's school day. Each original activity has been developed to focus on early childhood skills and concepts in inviting and playful ways.

Fine Motor: The ideas featured in the Fine Motor section provide big ideas for those little hands! You'll see crafts, centers, fingerplays, recipes, and skill-building ideas for language, science, and math. And each of those great ideas helps youngsters develop their small-muscle strength and coordination in fun and creative ways.

Movement: The Movement section features age-appropriate movement activities designed for indoor and outdoor play, and many require only minimal equipment. With these fun-to-use ideas, you're sure to watch your students' gross-motor skills improve by leaps and bounds!

Snacktime: The Snacktime pages feature clever recipes using an easy step-by-step format. Each recipe can be followed from start to finish with little or no help from the teacher. What a fun way to build youngsters' self-confidence! You'll be mixing important skills into your snacktime as youngsters develop their small-muscle coordination and work on measurement, counting, language skills, and much more.

We've conveniently made the recipe pages reproducible so you can copy, color, and laminate each one before placing it in your cooking area. Each recipe features a bonus idea to help you make the most of extra ingredients and add an extra helping of learning to your lesson.

Songs & Rhymes: Turn to the Songs & Rhymes section to find plenty of songs sung to popular tunes, fingerplays, and action rhymes—just right for little learners. Plus, you'll find many accompanying activities that use puppets, games, and props to help you introduce concepts and reinforce skills.

Storytime: Check out the suggested books and literature-based ideas the Storytime section has to offer. Five story recommendations for every theme provide lots of age-appropriate picture books to share. And, for each selection, you'll get a fresh idea for integrating learning and literature.

BUNNIES AND BASKETS

MATCHING BUNNY EARS

"Hare's" a matching activity that's sure to lead your little bunnies down the trail to skills development! To prepare, copy page 190 onto tagboard. Color the bunny, cut it out, and laminate it. Use a craft knife to make slits in the ears as indicated. Program the strips for the matching skill of your choice—uppercase and lowercase letters, numerals and dot sets, colors, or shapes. If desired, make multiple sets of strips and program as many different skills as desired. For ease of use, make each set of matching strips a different color. Laminate all the strips for durability.

To use this center, a child threads a set of strips through the ear slits as shown. She adjusts the strips to expose the matches. For an added challenge, provide paper and crayons and have kindergartners record each matched pair they find.

SOLID, STRIPES, SPOTS

Give your little ones "eggs-tra" practice in patterning using solid, striped, and spotted eggs. In advance, cut out a class supply of large oval eggs from white construction paper. Distribute the eggs; then invite each child to decorate his egg with a solid color, with stripes, or with spots. Then invite three youngsters—each with a different egg pattern—to stand side by side so that the class can see their eggs. Note the pattern created by the group. Then have more students join the line, repeating the pattern. Continue until the pattern can no longer be extended. Then start over, creating a different pattern. After several rounds, keep things hoppin' by inviting youngsters to direct themselves in creating patterns.

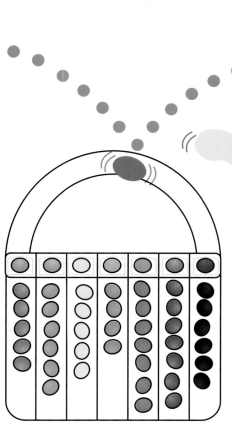

HOW MANY GREEN BEANS?

Your little bunnies will explore colors, graphing, and counting with this basketful of jelly beans. To prepare, gather a small-group supply of plastic eggs. Put ten jelly beans in each egg. Create a basket-shaped graph (as shown) on chart paper; then tape a different colored jelly bean to the top of each column. Place the graph on the floor and seat a small group of youngsters around it; then give each child an egg to open. Ask him to sort his jelly beans by color. Then have each child, in turn, place his jelly beans on the corresponding columns of the graph. Finally, recite the rhyme below to prompt the class to chorally count the jelly beans in each column. Repeat the rhyme, substituting a different jelly bean color each time. Then compare the results. Of which color are there the most jelly beans? The fewest? Are there the same number of any colors? Wow! This basket is full of learning!

[Green, green] jelly beans.
How many [green] beans have you seen?

BUNNIES THAT MEASURE UP

Perk up measuring, counting, and numeral-writing skills with the help of some bunny ears. To begin, copy the bunny pattern on page 190. Mask the ears on the copy; then enlarge and make four copies of the bunny face on pink construction paper. Cut out pairs of pink bunny ears in four different sizes. Laminate all the cutouts for durability. Put them in a center along with jelly beans and a wipe-off marker.

To use this center, a child gives each bunny face a pair of matching ears. She uses jelly beans to measure one ear in each pair from bottom to top. Then she counts the jelly beans and records the corresponding numeral on the other ear. After the child finishes with all four bunnies, invite her to eat the jelly beans she used for the activity. To prepare the pieces for the next child, simply wipe the numerals off the ears with a paper towel.

BUNNY ORDERS

Watch your little bunnies hop into action with this fun listen-and-do game. Provide each child with a plastic egg. Then recite the rhyme shown, filling in the blank with a positional phrase. Use a different phrase each time you repeat the rhyme. Then check to make sure "every-bunny" follows the directions correctly.

"Every-bunny" listen now
To what I have to say.
Place your egg [under a chair],
In a funny, bunny way.

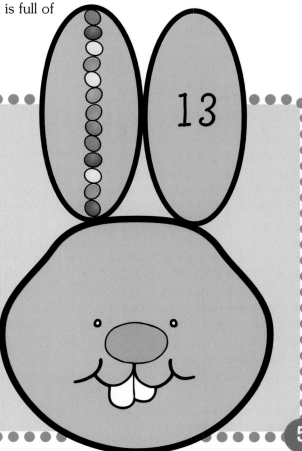

BUNNIES AND BASKETS

BUNCHES OF BUNNIES

"Hare's" an activity to get your little bunnies hoppin' to the art center to create their own bunnies. To prepare, supply the center with white paper doilies of two sizes, construction paper, a tagboard bunny-ear pattern, pink paper, pompoms, sticky dots, and short lengths of pipe cleaners. To create a bunny, a child glues a small and a large doily to a sheet of construction paper to form a bunny's head and body. He traces the ear pattern twice onto pink paper, then cuts out the ears and glues them to the bunny's head. He then attaches a pom-pom nose, two sticky-dot eyes, and pipe-cleaner whiskers to complete his bunny. This center is sure to be "rabbit-forming!"

SAND-FILLED EGGS

Your youngsters will get their fill of this "egg-citing" sand-table activity. Place a supply of colored plastic eggs in the sand table. Add plastic baskets for collecting eggs. Invite each student to fill some egg halves with sand, fit each with its corresponding half, and then collect the eggs in his basket. After all the eggs have been collected, ask youngsters to empty the contents of their eggs back into the sand table for the next group of bunnies. At a later time, you might have youngsters fill the eggs with toy critters, such as snakes, turtles, chicks, or other egg-hatching animals. Time to get cracking!

SEQUENCING STICKS

Challenge youngsters' sequencing skills with this math-center activity. To prepare, gather several sets of ten wide craft sticks and an assortment of ministickers, such as rabbits, eggs, and flowers. On each stick in a set, adhere a different number of identical stickers from one to ten. To prevent the stickers from peeling off, paint each stick with clear fingernail polish and let it dry. Then place each set of sticks in a separate basket. To use, invite student pairs to sequence the sticks in each set. Further challenge them to group together the sticks from each set having the same number of stickers. Then have the children return the stick sets to the baskets for the next pair.

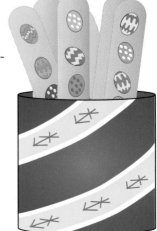

WONDERFUL WEAVES

Have your little hares hop over to the paint easel for a basketful of weaving fun. To prepare, cut a class supply of large construction-paper baskets. Then enlist the help of your little ones to tear different colors of construction paper into strips. Put the paper strips in a basket near the easel. Fill a paint pot with glue and add a paintbrush. Then clip a basket cutout to the easel. Show each little artist how to paint the cutout with glue and then add colorful strips of construction paper to create a basket weave. After the baskets are dry, have youngsters trim the excess paper from the basket edges. What wonderful weaves!

BUNNY BOX

Outfit youngsters with this prop-filled bunny box for some rabbit role-playing fun. In advance, collect bunny ears, baskets, a fancy hat, a bow tie or vest, and colored plastic eggs. Place the items in a cardboard box covered with Easter gift wrap; then put the box in your dramatic-play center. Invite youngsters to use the contents of the box as they role-play rabbit themes and schemes. Soon your little bunnies will be acting out their own "hoppily-ever-after" stories!

BUNNIES AND BASKETS

BUNNY WAND

Hop to it and create this adorable bunny wand! It's perfect to use as a pointer for reading songs, poems, and charts. Or wave it over your youngsters' heads and magically turn them into quiet little bunnies before you begin your circle time. Or pass it around during sharing time to indicate whose turn it is to talk.

To make a bunny wand, spray-paint a wooden spoon white. Cut bunny ears from white tagboard; then rub a cotton swab in powdered blush and add a bit of pink to the inside of the ears. Also from white tagboard, cut two bunny teeth. Then hot-glue the ears, teeth, two wiggle eyes, and a pink pom-pom nose onto the spoon as shown. If desired, tie a length of ribbon into a large bow and glue it to the spoon as a bow tie or a fancy hair bow.

COLORFUL EGGS

Send your little bunnies hoppin' on their way to stronger color-recognition skills with this colorful song. To prepare, collect enough colored plastic eggs for each child to have at least one. Have students sit in a circle; then place a basket in the center. Distribute the eggs and have each student identify the color of her egg. Then teach the song below. If a child has an egg that corresponds to the color in the song, have her hop to the basket and put her egg in. Continue with other colors until all your eggs are in one basket!

EGGS IN MY BASKET
(sung to the tune of "Skip to My Lou")

[Pink, <u>pink</u>, <u>pink</u>] little eggs.
[Pink, <u>pink</u>, <u>pink</u>] little eggs.
[Pink, <u>pink</u>, <u>pink</u>] little eggs.
[Pink] eggs in my basket.

BUNCHES OF BUNNIES

Get things hoppin' with this silly countdown rhyme. Have each child use his ten fingers to represent the ten little bunnies. Instruct each youngster to fold down one finger with each bunny that hops out of the basket.

(sung to the tune of "There Were Ten in the Bed")

Ten bunnies in the basket and the little one said,
Hop over! Hop over!
So they all hopped over,
And one hopped out.

(Continue counting down nine bunnies…eight bunnies…until you get to one bunny.)

One bunny in the basket and he sang out,

(sung to the tune of "He's Got the Whole World in His Hands")

"I've got the whole basket to myself.
I've got the whole basket to myself.
I've got the whole basket to myself.
I've got the whole basket to myself. Yippee!"

Ten bunnies in the basket and the little one said...

A-TISKET, A-TASKET, A NEW LEARNING BASKET

This alphabet activity is "eggs-actly" what you want to reinforce letter identification and sounds. Place a class supply of plastic eggs in a basket. Write each letter of the alphabet on an individual slip of paper; then put one letter inside each egg. (Or use magnetic or wooden alphabet letters instead.) Select one child to be the bunny; then have him hop about, distributing an egg to each child. Ask each youngster to open his egg, identify his letter, and name a word that begins with that letter sound. If desired, modify the activity to have children name a word with the same ending sound, name an object in the room that begins with the same sound, or find a matching alphabet letter in the print around the room. It's a basket of alphabet fun!

WHAT'S IN A NAME?

Combine each little one's name with this hip-hop chant that reinforces the sound of *H*. Substitute an *H* for the initial consonant in each child's name. If a child's name begins with an *H* (like Hannah), put an additional *H* at the beginning *(H-Hannah)*. Pause at the end of the last line to allow the child to shout out his name. Youngsters will find this name game h-hilarious!

Hippity, hoppity,
Hippity [H-ared].
Hippity, hoppity,
[His] name is…[Jared]!

BUNNIES AND BASKETS

SUSAN
HODNETT

FROM EGG BASKET TO EGG CARTON

Give little fingers an "eggs-tra" fine-motor workout at this center. Gather a basket of large pom-poms, several egg cartons, and a few pairs of tweezers. Invite small groups of students to visit the center. Have each child pick up one pom-pom "egg" at a time with the tweezers, then place it in an egg carton. Once his egg carton is full, have the child return the pom-poms to the basket. It just takes a pinch of practice for little ones to be successful at this task!

NEST EGGS

Crack open some fun with this nifty nesting activity! To prepare this center, collect colored plastic eggs in three sizes. Be sure each set of eggs has the same assortment of colors. Select an egg of the same color from each size set. To nest the eggs, put the small egg inside the medium egg; then put the medium egg inside the large egg. Separate the remaining eggs into halves; then put the egg halves in a large basket. Show students how the nested egg is put together. Invite each child who visits this center to sort the egg halves by color; then have him nest three sizes of each egg color together. When he is done, have him take the eggs apart so the next child can try his hand at some nesting fun.

SEASONAL SEWING

This center is the place to lace! To prepare, purchase Easter or spring-themed bulletin board decorations in simple shapes, as well as long shoelaces in spring colors or seasonal prints. Punch holes around the edge of each bulletin board piece. Thread one end of a shoelace through one hole in each piece, then tie it. Place the resulting sewing cards in a center. Encourage each youngster at this center to select a card; then have her sew the lace through the holes. Fine-motor practice is "sew" much fun!

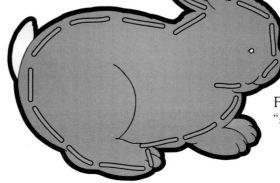

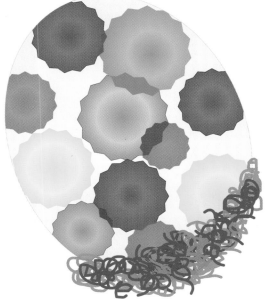

EXTRAORDINARY EGGS

Drip, drop, the fun won't stop when your little ones make these colorful eggs. To set up an egg-making station, gather coffee filters, paper towels, glue, and Easter grass. Then cut a class supply of construction paper ovals similar in size to a flattened coffee filter. Fill several muffin-tin cups with water; then use food coloring to tint each cup of water a different spring color. Put an eyedropper in each cup of colored water. To make an egg, flatten a coffee filter on top of a paper towel. Squeeze several drops of each water color onto the filter. After the filter dries, glue it to a paper oval and trim it to an oval shape; then glue some green Easter grass to one end of the egg.

To display these crafty eggs, attach a large construction paper basket to your bulletin board. Then watch youngsters' "egg-citement" build as you fill the basket with their colorful eggs.

TEAR A HARE

Youngsters are guaranteed to have a rip-roarin' time when they make these adorable bunnies! In advance, gather glue, 12" x 18" sheets of white construction paper, and construction paper scraps in a variety of colors (including black and pink). To make a bunny, a child tears a large bunny body and a small bunny head from white paper. She tears white paper strips to represent the bunny's ears and legs. Then she glues the bunny's body together. She adds details—such as black whiskers or pink ears—by tearing the colored paper scraps and then gluing them in place. What a "tear-rific" hare!

11

BUNNIES AND BASKETS

BUNNY HOP

Come along for some hip-hoppin' fun down the bunny trail! Encourage each of your little bunnies to hop on both feet with paws held close to his chest. Invite youngsters to hop high, low, fast, slow, in a circle, on one foot, etc. Ask little ones to take giant hops forward and bitsy bunny hops backward. Then have them hop from one designated area to another, counting the number of hops it takes to get there. Hip! Hop! Once you start, you can't stop!

HOOP IT UP!

Do your youngsters have as much energy as the Energizer Bunny®? Then try the Hoop Hip-Hop. First lay a course of plastic hoops on the floor with rims touching. Demonstrate how to hop on two feet into each hoop. Encourage each child to hop through the entire course once. Then divide the class into small groups. Collect the hoops, and then arrange an equal number of hoops on the floor for each group. Give your little bunnies more chances to do the Hoop Hip-Hop.

HIP-HOP BASKET BOP

Have a basketful of fun as your youngsters bebop with baskets. In advance ask each child to bring a basket from home. In an open area, instruct each youngster to stand with her basket on the floor. Make certain there is adequate space between each child. Challenge each child to move around her basket in a variety of ways. After the youngsters have exhausted their own ideas, use a basket to demonstrate various actions your students can try. Show how to step over the basket and gallop around it. Take giant steps with the basket behind your back or on your head. Have a hip-hoppin', basket-boppin' time!

susan
Hodnett

"E-RACER" RABBIT

Show your little magicians how to make a rabbit disappear! Lay a plastic liner on the floor near your chalkboard; then place a few small containers of water on the liner. Cut some sponges into quarters. Then draw several simple line drawings of rabbits on the chalkboard. Make the drawings large with ample space between the rabbits. Demonstrate for the class how to wet a sponge, then squeeze out the excess water into a container. Illustrate how to use large arm movements with the sponge to erase the chalk lines of one rabbit outline. Invite a few children at a time to make the rabbits disappear as fast as they can say "Abracadabra!"

EGG ROLL

Get those bunny tails in high gear for some "eggs-ercise"! Collect a colored plastic egg for each child. In an open space outdoors, lay two ropes several feet apart on the ground to designate the beginning and end of a bunny trail. Give each little bunny an egg; then challenge her to move the egg from one end of the trail to the other. Encourage youngsters to kick their eggs down the trail or push the eggs along with their thumbs, elbows, or noses. Congratulate each bunny for her "egg-ceptional" effort.

BUNNIES AND BASKETS

BUNNY CAKE

Ingredients:
1 cupcake per child
white frosting
jelly beans
minimarshmallows
string licorice
1 Keebler® Cookie Stix™ cookie (or other stick-
   shaped cookie) per child

Utensils and Supplies:
1 plastic knife (or craft stick) per child
napkins

Teacher Preparation:
   Prepare a class supply of cupcakes in paper
baking cups. Cut six 1 1/2-inch lengths of string
licorice for each child. Cut one Keebler® Cookie
Stix™ in half per child. Arrange the ingredients
and utensils near the step-by-step direction cards.

WHAT TO DO WHEN
THE SNACK IS THROUGH

   Can your little bunnies identify a jelly bean by using
only their sense of taste? Try this simple jelly-bean
taste test to find out. Display one jelly bean of each
color in front of the class. Direct a student volunteer to
close his eyes. Place a leftover jelly bean in his hand
and have him keep his eyes closed while he eats it.
Then ask him to view the jelly-bean lineup and point
to the color he tasted. Invite your entire bunch of
bunnies to put their taste buds to this test.

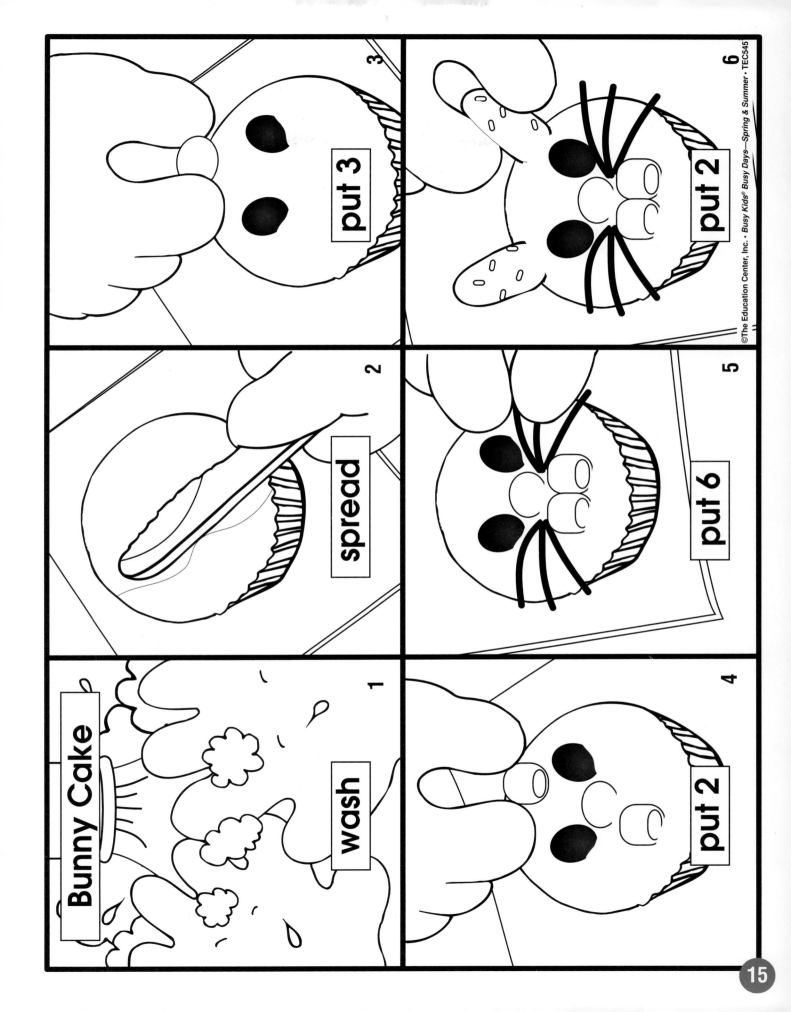

Bunny Cake

wash **1**

spread **2**

put 3 **3**

put 2 **4**

put 6 **5**

put 2 **6**

BUNNIES AND BASKETS

LITTLE BITTY BUNNY

(sung to the tune of "Little Rabbit Foo-Foo")

Little bitty bunny,	*Show fist with two fingers tall.*
Hopping through the garden,	*Hop bunny up and down.*
Nibblin' at the lettuce	*With fists together, wiggle bunny ears.*
And eating the farmer's crop!	*Rub tummy.*
Then out came the angry farmer	*Cross arms and look mad.*
And he said,	
"Little bitty bunny,	*Shake finger.*
I don't think you're funny,	*Shake head and finger.*
Nibblin' at my lettuce	
And eating up my crop!	
I'll give you [three chances].	*Hold up three fingers.*
If you don't stop eating my garden	*Shake finger.*
I'll turn you into a stew!"	*Make stirring motion.*

But the next day:

(Repeat two more times, replacing the underlined words with two more chances *and then with* one more chance. *Hold up the appropriate number of fingers each time.)*

Little bitty bunny,	*Show fist with two fingers tall.*
Hopping through the garden,	*Hop bunny up and down.*
Nibblin' at the lettuce	*With fists together, wiggle bunny ears.*
And eating the farmer's crop!	*Rub tummy.*
Then out came the angry farmer	*Cross arms and look mad.*
And he said,	
"Little bitty bunny,	*Shake finger.*
I don't think you're funny,	*Shake head and finger.*
Nibblin' at my lettuce	
And eating up my crop!	
I gave you three chances.	*Hold up three fingers.*
Now I'm turning you into a stew!"	*Make stirring motion.*

(Finish the song by reciting the rhyme below.)

But the farmer's daughter said,	
"Please don't turn this bunny into a stew!	*Shake head.*
I've got an idea! I know what to do!	*Tap temple with forefinger.*
Bunny, take this carrot to munch.	*Pretend to hold out carrot.*
And next time, wait till you're *invited* to lunch!"	*Shake finger.*

I'M AN EASTER BASKET

(sung to the tune of "I'm a Little Teapot")

I'm an Easter basket
Stuffed with treats,
Like chocolate bunnies
And other sweets!

I'll make someone happy,
Gosh, oh gee,
When the Easter bunny
Delivers me!

HIPPITY-HOPPITY

(sung to the tune of "Here Comes Peter Cottontail")

Here comes Bop-pi-ty Bunny,
Hoppin' a-long so funny,
Hippity-hoppity,
Spring is on its way!

Hoppin' through the fields so
    green,
Sniffing every flower seen,
Hippity-hoppity,
Spring is here to stay!

BUNNY TICKLES ME

Tickle youngsters' funny-bunny bones with this silly song. If desired, use a washable marker to draw a bunny face at the base of each child's index and tall finger. Then have the child hold up the two fingers to represent bunny ears. Invite him to hop his bunny to the body part named in the song. Then have him tickle that body part with his bunny ears. Each time you repeat the song, name a different body part.

(adapted to the verse of "Skip to My Lou")

Hop, hop, hop to my [knee],
Hop, hop, hop to my [knee],
Hop, hop, hop to my [knee],
Hop to my [knee], my bunny.

Bunny tickles me. Shoo, bunny, shoo!

Bunny tickles me. Shoo, bunny, shoo!
Bunny tickles me. Shoo, bunny, shoo!
Hop away, my bunny!

Hop bunny to body part.

*Tickle with bunny ears.
Shoo bunny away.*

Hop bunny behind back.

BUNNIES AND BASKETS

RABBIT'S GOOD NEWS

Watch your little bunnies' ears perk right up for a reading of *Rabbit's Good News* by Ruth Lercher Bornstein (Clarion Books). The soft and warm pastel illustrations are a natural invitation for your children to make some pastel pictures of their own. To prepare, make several tagboard cutouts of the bunny on page 191. Place the cutouts in your art center, along with markers, white paper, tape, and large sticks of colored chalk in soft colors. Instruct a child to lay a sheet of paper over a bunny cutout; then tape the paper to the table. Have her use the side of a piece of chalk to make a rubbing over the bunny. Encourage her to blend other colors of chalk around the bunny. As a final touch, have her use markers to add facial features. Add a spritz of hairspray to prevent the chalk from rubbing off. It's bunny magic!

LaQueeta

LITTLE BUNNY'S EASTER SURPRISE

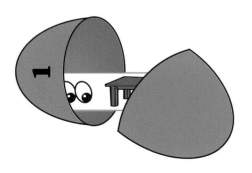

There are all kinds of surprises in store when you read *Little Bunny's Easter Surprise* by Jeanne Modesitt (Simon & Schuster Books for Young Readers). After sharing the story, treat your little ones to a surprise treasure hunt similar to the one in the story. First, create a number of clues (like the one shown) to help your youngsters locate a hidden surprise. Place each clue inside a numbered plastic egg. Set aside egg number one; then put egg number two in the location dictated by the clue in egg number one. Continue to hide the eggs in the appropriate places, so that little ones can follow the clues. Hide a basket of treats—such as a class supply of plastic eggs with jelly beans inside—at the final location.

To begin the hunt, divide your class into the same number of small groups as the number of clues. Give one group egg number one and have group members decipher the clue inside. After the group has searched and found the next egg, have another group follow the directions on the second clue. Continue in this fashion until the last group has discovered the basket. Your little bunnies will be hip-hoppin' with delight to discover their surprise!

THE SPRING RABBIT

When Smudge gets tired of waiting for a brother or sister bunny to arrive, he decides to make his own in *The Spring Rabbit* by Joyce Dunbar (Bantam Books). After reading the story, invite your youngsters to make these unique bunnies from clay and natural materials. First take the class on a nature walk. Invite youngsters to gather twigs, leaves, pine needles, or other small nature items. After returning to the classroom, give each child some clay or play dough. Have the class follow your lead as you mold a portion of clay into a bunny. Roll a small portion of the clay between your hands to form a ball. Roll another larger ball, and then mold them together to form the bunny's head and body. Then shape and attach two long ears to the head. Encourage each child to use his collected nature items to decorate his clay bunny.

THE EASTER EGG ARTISTS

Stress the importance of individuality as you read aloud *The Easter Egg Artists* by Adrienne Adams (Aladdin Paperbacks). Young Orson Abbott was encouraged to develop his own painting style. Do the same for your youngsters by giving them an opportunity to experiment with various painting tools and techniques. Provide new, various-sized paintbrushes as well as other clean painting tools, such as toothbrushes, sponges, cotton swabs, cotton balls, rollers, and feathers. Give each child a small container of water. Invite each child to use the water and painting tools to "water-paint" chalkboards, tabletops, or sidewalks. Encourage him to try making various brush strokes, such as swirls, lines, and zigzags. After ample time for experimentation, give each child a large oval egg cut from tagboard and invite him to use real paints to design an original Easter egg. Compliment each of your young artists on his unique painting style.

THE COUNTRY BUNNY AND THE LITTLE GOLD SHOES

Learn how kindness is rewarded in *The Country Bunny and the Little Gold Shoes* by Du Bose Heyward (Houghton Mifflin Company). After reading this timeless classic (in two sessions for younger listeners), discuss the things that earned Mother Cottontail the golden shoes—her kindness, speed, wisdom, and bravery. Tell youngsters that these qualities deserve to be rewarded, and then show them a small basket. Explain that a jelly bean will be placed in the basket each time a child exhibits one of these qualities. When the basket has a jelly bean for every child, reward the class by making golden shoes like the ones Mother Cottontail received.

Use the pattern on page 191 to cut out a pair of tagboard shoes for each child; then place the cutouts on a newspaper-covered table, along with diluted glue, paintbrushes, gold glitter, yarn, and a hole puncher. Help the child punch a hole in the top of her pair of tagboard shoes. Thread a length of yarn through the hole and tie the ends together to make a necklace. Have the child paint glue onto her tagboard shoes and then sprinkle them with gold glitter. Once they are dry, invite the child to wear the golden shoes around her neck as a reminder of her fine qualities.

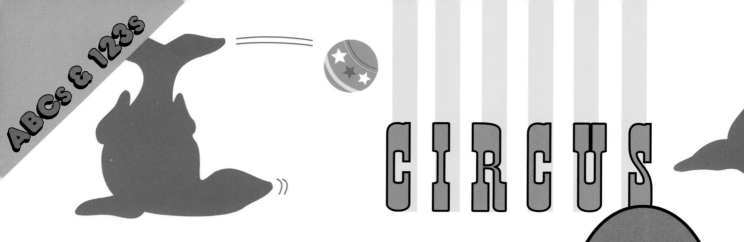

CIRCUS

Colorful Clown Hair

Entice youngsters to clown around with this activity focusing on colors and color words. Draw a simple clown head as shown. Duplicate the drawing onto several sheets of white construction paper; then color each clown's facial features, but not the hair. Label each bow tie with a color word, such as *red, yellow,* or *purple.* (For younger students, use corresponding markers to write the color words.) Laminate the clowns; then place them in a center with food coloring, shaving cream, paper towels, and paintbrushes.

A child at this center squirts some shaving cream onto a clown's hair. She finds the food coloring (or color combination) corresponding to the color word on the bow tie and then squeezes a few drops onto the shaving cream. She blends the color into the shaving cream with a paintbrush and then paints the clown's hair with the mixture. She paints the hair on the other clowns in a similar fashion. Then she wipes the hair colors off with a paper towel to prepare the center for the next clown-hair stylist.

green

Dane the clown walked a tightrope today! It was <u>12</u> clown feet long.

Big Shoes to Fill

Step right into some measurement practice with the help of some clown shoes. Visit your local party-supply store and purchase a pair of clown shoes. Draw the outline of a clown shoe on paper; then program the outline with "_____ the clown walked a tightrope today! It was _____ clown feet long." Duplicate a class supply of the shoe pattern onto red construction paper. Then stretch a long rope across the floor. Invite each child, in turn, to put on the shoes. Have her walk the "tightrope" heel-to-toe as she counts each step. Help her record her name and the number of steps taken on her shoe pattern. Then instruct her to cut out her pattern. (If desired, you might photograph each child's clown act; then attach the photo to the back of her cutout.) Encourage each child to share her results with her family to show how she measures up as a clown!

Animal Cracker Circus

Students are bound to go crackers over this sorting activity. In advance, purchase a large box of animal crackers. Program each of several large index cards with the first letter of the name of an animal represented in the box. For younger students, glue the animal crackers whose names begin with that letter onto the card and write the animal name below each one. Place the cards, animal crackers, and napkins in a center. Ask each visitor to count out ten crackers onto a napkin. Have her sort the crackers by matching either the animal-name beginning sounds or the actual animal crackers. Then invite her to munch those yummy crackers for a circus snack!

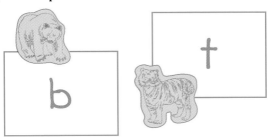

Get Your Peanuts Here!

Shell out opportunities to strengthen estimating skills with a bag of peanuts. To prepare, color red stripes on a white lunch bag so that it resembles a circus peanut bag. Use pinking shears to cut the bag so that it is only about five inches tall. Seat students in a circle; then give each child a handful of unshelled peanuts. Ask each child to estimate how many peanuts it will take to fill the bag. Write each child's estimate beside her name on a sheet of chart paper. Then pass the bag around the circle. Ask the class to count together as each child drops one peanut into the bag. Continue until the bag is full. Record the final number on the chart paper; then have youngsters compare their estimates to the actual number.

What's Under the Big Top?

Help your kindergartners improve their beginning-sounds skills as they explore what's under the big top. Draw a simple circus tent, as shown, on a large sheet of red construction paper. Then cut out simple circus pictures from coloring books or magazines. Glue each cutout onto the left side of a sentence strip. Then, substituting a blank for the first letter of each word, label each strip. For self-checking purposes, write the missing letter on the back of each strip. Laminate the strips and the tent picture for durability; then staple the top edge of the tent picture to a large sheet of tagboard. Place the strips under the big top; then put the big top in a center with a wipe-off marker. To use, the child lifts the big top to remove a word strip. He fills in the missing letter and then checks his work. After he completes the activity, he wipes off the strips and then places them under the big top for the next child.

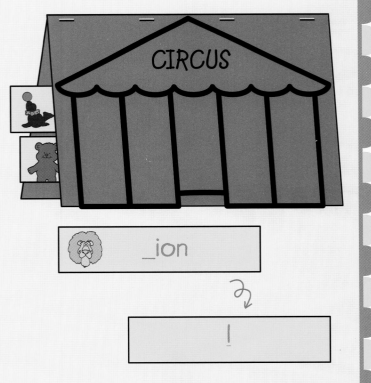

21

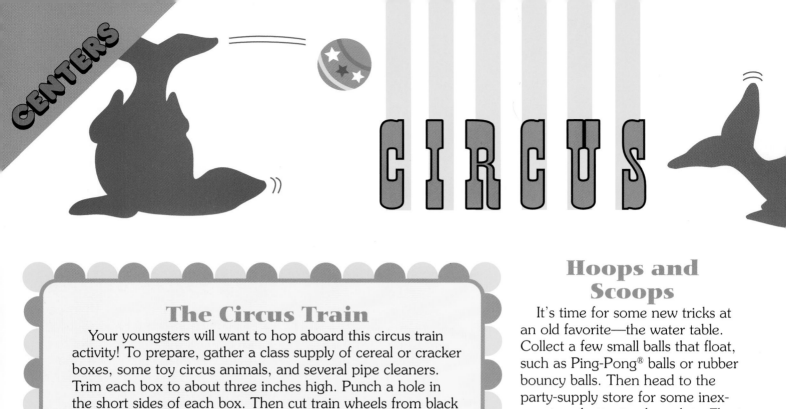

CIRCUS

The Circus Train

Your youngsters will want to hop aboard this circus train activity! To prepare, gather a class supply of cereal or cracker boxes, some toy circus animals, and several pipe cleaners. Trim each box to about three inches high. Punch a hole in the short sides of each box. Then cut train wheels from black construction paper.

Have each child paint a box with a color of his choice. When the boxes are dry, have him glue construction paper wheels to his box train car. To assemble the cars into a train, have youngsters connect them with pipe cleaner halves. Finally, invite the children to load up the train with animals, then chug on over to the dramatic-play center or the block center for some imaginative play.

Hoops and Scoops

It's time for some new tricks at an old favorite—the water table. Collect a few small balls that float, such as Ping-Pong® balls or rubber bouncy balls. Then head to the party-supply store for some inexpensive plastic ring bracelets. Float the bracelets in the water and encourage your young circus performers to drop balls into the hoops from different levels. Add scoops and cups to the bracelets and balls, and your little ones will no doubt invent some new tricks of their own!

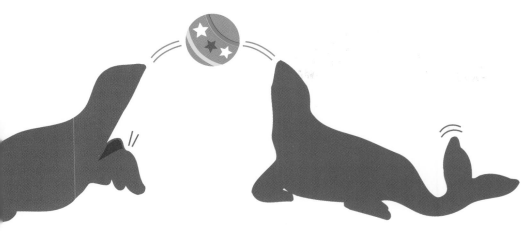

Under the Big Top

Turn your block area into an amazing three-ring circus. Put three plastic hoops on the floor of the block area to define workspaces. Gather toys and other items to represent circus characters and props, such as toy animals and people, dollhouse chairs, and ring bracelets. Present these items to the class, encouraging the children to brainstorm how these and other things in the room might be used to create imaginary circus acts. For example, the chairs might be used as lion-taming tools, while the bracelets might serve as jumping hoops for circus dogs. Then place the circus props in the block area. Assign one child at a time to each plastic hoop; then invite him to create a circus act inside his "ring." If desired, take instant photos of each act. Display the photographs in the block area to ignite the imaginations of the rest of your little ringmasters.

Estimation Sensation

Youngsters will be more than willing to pop into your sensory center for this estimating activity. Send each child home with a note requesting that each family send in a bag of cooked popcorn. Empty the bags into your sensory table; then add scoops and some paper lunch bags. Explain to youngsters that this popcorn is to play with—not to eat! Then have visitors to the center estimate the number of popcorn scoops needed to fill a bag. Invite each child to count the actual number of scoops needed, then compare that amount with her estimate. After all your little ones have enjoyed this circus attraction, scatter the popcorn outdoors as a treat for the birds. Then serve youngsters a freshly popped batch of popcorn at snacktime.

Clown "Mask–erades"

Send your little ones to the art center to make funny masks for clowning around. In advance, inflate and knot a class supply of small, round balloons. Then prepare a mask for each child by cutting two eyeholes and a nosehole in a paper plate. Staple a craft stick to the plate to serve as a handle. Place the balloons, masks, and an assortment of construction paper shapes in the art center. Encourage each child to create a clown mask by gluing paper-shape features—such as ears, hair, and accessories—onto the plate. Then help her attach a silly balloon nose to her mask by pulling the knotted end of a balloon through the nosehole and securing it with tape. Invite your little clowns to don their silly masks for a few laughs in your dramatic-play center.

Note: Balloons can be a choking hazard for small children. Provide close supervision.

CIRCUS

Nuts About Elephants

Reinforce counting skills as your little animal trainers prepare to feed some hungry elephants. In advance put ten unshelled peanuts in a zippered plastic bag for every two students in your group. Divide your group into pairs. Designate one child in each pair as the elephant, and give him a paper cup. Designate the other child as the trainer and give her the bag of peanuts. After reciting the chant below, ask one elephant to call out a number. Then have each trainer count that number of peanuts from her bag into her elephant's cup. Do a quick check of the cups and assist with the counting as necessary; then have the elephants return the peanuts to the bags before repeating the chant and having another elephant call out a number. After a few rounds, have the elephants and trainers switch places.

Elephant, Elephant raise your trunk high—
Way, way up to the sky.
How many peanuts for you today?
How many nuts can you stow away?

Jumbo Fun for Everyone

Give your little elephant trainers some estimating practice with this "pea-nutty" activity. Provide each youngster with an unshelled peanut. Invite each child to guess how many nuts are in his shell; then record his response. Invite all your little ones to open their peanuts, check their guesses, and then have a nutty time eating them! Challenge students further by providing two more peanuts for each child. Knowing how many peanuts were in one shell, can your little ones estimate how many peanuts will be in two shells?

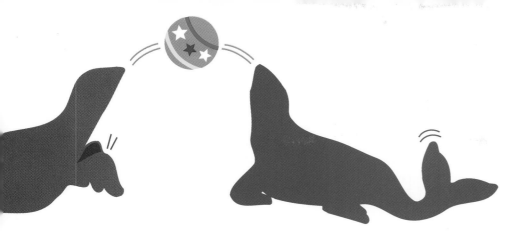

Bring On the Clowns

Your youngsters are sure to fancy the funny faces in this visual-discrimination activity. To prepare, cut a clown's facial features and accessories (such as a bow tie or hat) from colorful felt. Cut enough features for two clown faces, making them different in shape and color. During circle time, use the felt cutouts to make a clown face on your flannelboard—excluding an *eye*, a *nose*, or another feature. Ask the children to determine what is missing from the clown. Continue by interchanging the felt pieces to make new faces. Or put features where they don't belong on the clown; then ask youngsters to identify what's wrong. Invite little ones to use the felt pieces to make their own crazy clown characters during free play.

Come Clown Around

Invite your youngsters to clown around with this panto-mime performance. Teach youngsters the following song; then have them suggest things a clown might do in his circus act—such as make funny faces, ride a unicycle, or juggle balls. Encourage little ones to act out each suggested clown antic as they sing the song with you.

(sung to the tune of
"The Bear Went Over the Mountain")

Come clown around in the circus,
Come clown around in the circus,
Come clown around in the circus,
And entertain the crowd!

Circus Circle of Fun!

Capture that big-top feeling during circle time by creating your very own three-ring circus! To prepare, place three plastic hoops or circles made from string on the floor. Invite three children to stand in the rings and perform a circus act, such as reciting the alphabet, counting to 20, or singing a special song. Have all three children perform the same act together. Introduce the performers as you announce the act with fanfare. You might say, "Ladies and gentlemen, let me present [Joey, Kaley, and Erin] singing 'The Clown Song.'" After the performance, encourage three more performers to get into the act!

CIRCUS

I'm a Clown!

Make 'em laugh with these personalized clown puppets that are sure to win over any audience. In advance, take a close-up photo of each child; then carefully cut out the child's face in each developed picture. Prepare several tagboard-tracer sets so that each set includes a large triangle, a small triangle, a long rectangle, and a short rectangle. Put the face cutouts, the tracer sets, construction paper, sticky dots, paper fasteners, and glue in your art center.

To create a puppet, a child traces onto construction paper a large triangle (the body), a small triangle (the hat), two short rectangles (the arms), and two long rectangles (the legs). He cuts out each shape. Then he attaches the arms and legs to the body with paper fasteners as shown. Next, he glues his head cutout to the body, then glues the hat onto his head. Finally, he decorates his clown with sticky dots and construction paper features of his choice, such as a bow tie, a collar, or shoes. When the clowns are complete, invite each child to move his clown along to this song:

(sung to the tune of "I've Been Working on the Railroad")

This clown works at the circus
All the livelong day.
This clown works at the circus
Having fun in silly ways.
See the funny clown dancing.
Now watch him wave to you.
See the funny clown standing
On his silly head for you!

Play Dough Clowns

Youngsters will be rolling with laughter when they roll out these comical play dough clowns. Set up your play dough center with colorful play dough, shape cookie cutters, buttons, colored macaroni, feathers, and pipe cleaners. Also, add rolling pins, plastic knives, and a garlic press to the center. Then invite each child to visit the center to create a clown. Have her cut cookie-cutter shapes from play dough for the clown's body parts, such as a square tummy and a round head. Then encourage her to add features to her clown, such as pipe cleaner arms and legs, button eyes, and a macaroni mouth (positioned to make a happy or a sad clown). Invite her to use dough run through the garlic press or colorful feathers for hair. These crazy clowns are sure to get your group giggling!

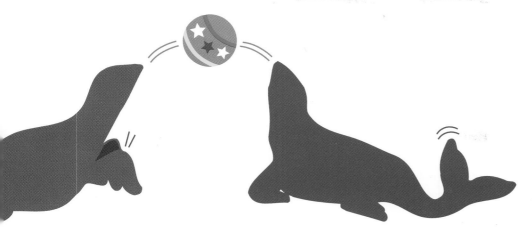

Squirt the Clown

Step right up to the water table for this game of chance and skill. To prepare, use permanent markers to draw clown faces onto a desired number of white Styrofoam® plates. Be sure to draw a large mouth on each clown; then cut a quarter-sized hole in the center of each mouth. Put the clown plates into your water table, along with some turkey basters or squeeze bottles. Cover the floor beneath the table with a vinyl tablecloth or—better yet—move the table outdoors for this activity. Invite each child at this center to fill a turkey baster or squirt bottle with water. Then have her squirt water into the hole in each clown's mouth. For an added challenge, encourage the child to aim and squirt the water from different distances. Now that's a mouthful of wet and wild fun!

Tricks of the Trade

Challenge your young performers to try their hands at this neat disappearing act. Invite a student volunteer to assume the role of a circus performer. Have her stand in front of the group; then place a half-sheet of paper at her feet. Have her place one hand behind her back; then encourage her to pick up the paper with her other hand. Challenge her to use only that hand to crumple the paper into a small ball that "disappears" inside her fist. Once the paper disappears, have the child victoriously say, "Abracadabra!" and bow to an applauding audience. Later, invite your little performers to attempt this feat using other materials, such as aluminum foil, waxed paper, or a sponge. For a crowd-pleasing finale, ask each brave little one to repeat this act using her other hand.

The Circus Is Coming to Town!

Here's a way to bring the circus to your youngsters' fingertips. Duplicate a few simple circus pictures from a clip art or pattern book (or draw your own). Tape the circus pictures to a classroom window at a child's eye level. (If you do not have a window, tape the pictures to a tabletop.) Put washable markers, tape, and tracing paper near the circus scenes. On a sunny day, encourage each of your circus fans to tape a piece of tracing paper over her favorite circus picture. With the sun shining through the picture to provide a clear outline, have her carefully trace over the scene. Help her carefully remove the tracing paper to see the circus appear right before her eyes! Invite her to use markers to add some color and details to her circus scene.

CIRCUS

Juggling Time

Step right up to the greatest show on earth—featuring your own junior jugglers! Give each child a scarf (or a beanbag) so he can practice his juggling act. Put on some music and encourage each juggler to try the movements below. It's an activity your youngsters won't want to toss away!

- Toss the scarf up, and catch it with the same hand.
- Toss the scarf up, and catch it with the opposite hand.
- Toss the scarf up, and then clap and catch it.

For the juggler who's ready to wow the crowd:

- Toss the scarf up, turn around, and then catch it.
- Toss the scarf up, and then catch it on your arm, shoe, back, etc.

Tots on a Tightrope

Rope your youngsters in with this next act—a balancing act on the tightrope! For a high wire, use a balance beam or adhere a long strip of tape to the floor. Give each of your little circus performers a beanbag or a wooden block. Ask each child to balance her object on her hand, head, or foot. Then demonstrate how to balance the same object on your head while walking forward, backward, or sideways on the high wire. Now it's down to the wire, so let your little ones have a try. Ready? Steady? Go!

Elephant Feeding Frenzy

What to feed the elephants? Peanuts, of course! In advance, hide peanuts (in their shells) around your classroom or playground. Draw or cut out a picture of an elephant and tape it to a bucket. Then pass out a plastic spoon to each child. Tell your little animal trainers that the elephants are hungry and need your help gathering their food; then send them on a hunt for peanuts. Explain that once a hidden peanut is found, it must be placed on a spoon and carried to the elephant's bucket. When the hunt is over, invite your children to pretend to be hungry elephants. Have them give the peanuts a crack and eat them for a snack!

Send in the Clowns!

Invite your little ones to clown around as they perform the clown tricks described below. Provide floor mats or carpeting to cushion your comical characters.

Log roll: lie on side; then roll over like a log

Head/toe touch: lie on stomach; then support upper body on hands (with elbows straight); touch toes to head

Rocking horse: lie on stomach; catch ankles with hands; then rock back and forth from chest to knees

Ball roll: draw knees to chest while sitting; then lock arms around knees; roll over and around like a ball

Somersault: sit on knees; put chin to chest; roll over headfirst

Bridge: lie on back with palms flat on the floor beside head; push up with hands and feet

Clowning Around

Enjoy some silly clown antics as you sing the following song. Select a child to demonstrate a silly movement or a funny face; then invite your little clowns to mime her actions. Encourage all youngsters to take turns being the lead clown.

(sung to the tune of "Did You Ever See a Lassie?")

Did you ever see a clo-wn, a clo-wn, a clo-wn,
Did you ever see a clo-wn act silly like this?
Act silly like this and act silly like that?
Oh! Did you ever see a clo-wn act silly like this?

CIRCUS

Clown Hat

Ingredients:
1 sugar cone per child
white frosting
round, berry-flavored cereal (such as Cap'n Crunch's
    Oops! All Berries™)
1 red maraschino cherry per child

Utensils and Supplies:
1 plastic knife (or craft stick) per child
spoon
napkins

Teacher Preparation:
    Drain the cherries; then remove the stems.
Arrange the ingredients and utensils near the step-
by-step direction cards.

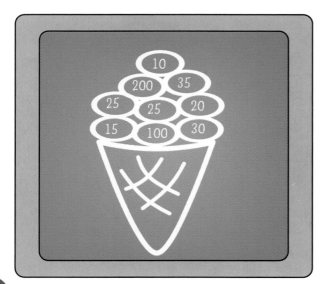

What to Do When the Snack Is Through

Challenge your little ones to estimate the number of leftover berry cereal pieces it will take to fill an ice-cream cone. If desired, draw an ice-cream cone on the chalkboard. Write each child's estimate in a circle above the cone. Then have youngsters count along as you fill the real cone with one piece of cereal at a time. Discuss which estimates were closest to the actual number.

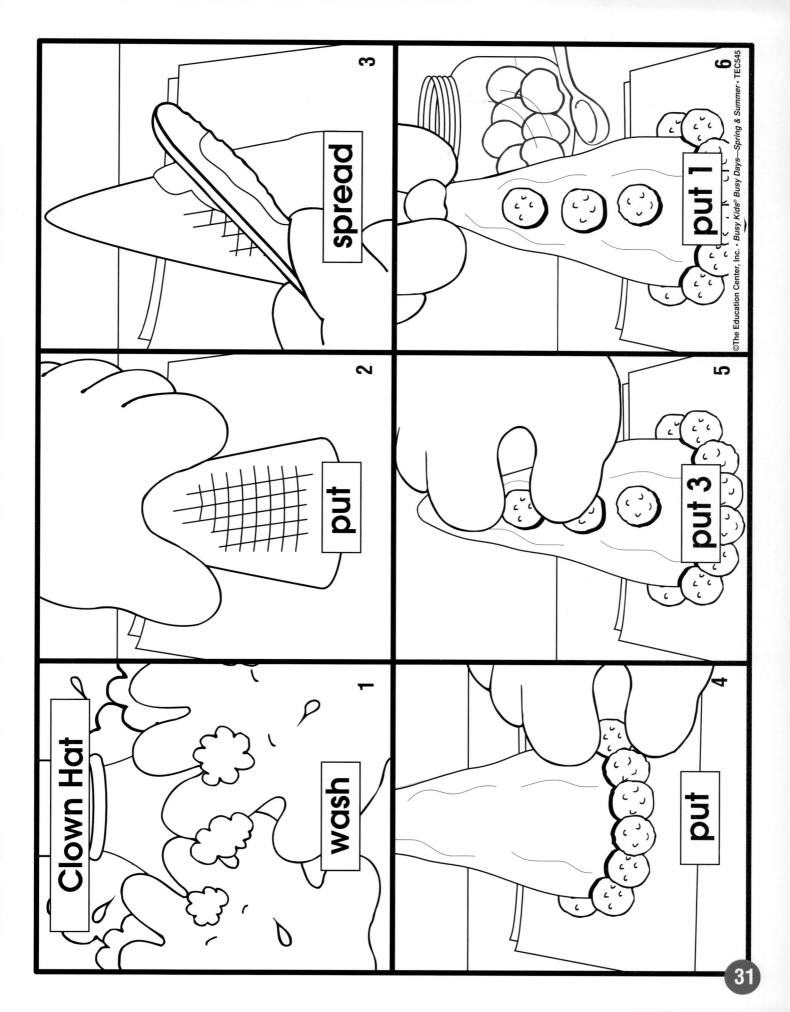

Clown Hat

wash 1

put 2

spread 3

put 4

put 3 5

put 1 6

CIRCUS

Clown Capers

Introduce your youngsters to multiple fun when you clown around with this counting rhyme. Encourage little ones to hold up the appropriate number of fingers as they sing along.

(sung to the tune of "The Ants Go Marching")

The clowns come running one by one.
Hurrah! Hurrah!
The clowns come running one by one.
Hurrah! Hurrah!
The clowns come running one by one,
The little one stops to have some fun.
And they all go running
Into the tent to begin the big show. Oh! Oh! Oh!

The clowns come running
    two by two.
The little one stops to tie
    his shoe.

The clowns come running
    three by three.
The little one stops to
    laugh, "Hee! Hee!"

The clowns come running
    four by four.
The little one stops when
    the lions roar!

The clowns come running
    five by five.
The little one stops to flip
    and dive.

Going to the Circus

(sung to the tune of "Did You Ever See a Lassie?")

We're going to the circus,
The circus, the circus.
We're going to the circus.
Would you like to come?

There are lions and tigers,
And bareback horse riders.
We're going to the circus.
Would you like to come?

We're going to the circus,
The circus, the circus.
We're going to the circus.
Would you like to come?

There are acrobats on wires,
And jugglers with fire.
We're going to the circus.
Would you like to come?

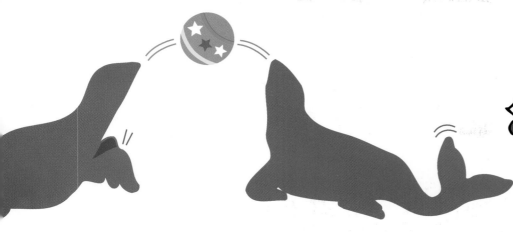

The Circus Is Coming
(sung to the tune of "I've Been Working on the Railroad")

I've been waiting for the circus,
So many long, long days.
I've been waiting for the circus,
And it's coming here today!

Hear the ringmaster a-calling,
"Ladies and Gentlemen!"
Hear the audience a-chanting,
"Let the show begin!"

Lions will roar,
Acrobats soar,
Silly clowns parade around and
  round.

Horses will prance,
Bears ride and dance,
It's the best show in town!

Five Acrobats

   Practice counting down with this adaptation of the traditional chant "Five Little Monkeys Jumping on the Bed." As you begin each verse, encourage each youngster to show the correct number of fingers to represent the acrobats. Then have him swoop one finger through the air to illustrate an acrobat swooping down from the sky.

Five acrobats flying oh-so-high.
One swooped down out of the sky.
A funny circus clown who was walking by,
Caught the acrobat, saying, "My, oh my!"

Four acrobats…
Three acrobats…
Two acrobats…

One acrobat flying oh-so-high.
He swooped down out of the sky.
A funny circus clown who was
  walking by,
Caught him and said, "Glad I don't
  fly!"

33

CIRCUS

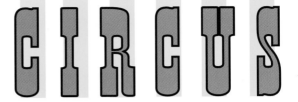

Ginger Jumps

Your circus audience will be on the edge of their seats rooting for Ginger, the circus dog, in *Ginger Jumps* by Lisa Campbell Ernst (Aladdin Paperbacks). After sharing the story, invite your youngsters to portray circus dogs and practice some gross-motor skills at the same time. First, have each child cut two triangles from brown construction paper. Have her glue the two triangles—dog ears—to a sentence strip headband. Then, with her doggie disguise in place, introduce her to the class, giving her a name that will indicate her circus talent. For example, you might introduce Louis, the Jumping Dog, or Mary Kate, the Skipping Dog. As each of your little ones "bow-wows" the audience, reward her with a treat—such as a cracker or small cookie.

This is Danielle, the Prancing Dog!

LUKe

In the third circus ring, my class saw with me three clowns acting silly.

The Twelve Circus Rings

Clown around with numbers in *The Twelve Circus Rings* by Seymour Chwast (Harcourt Brace & Company). This zany adaptation of "The Twelve Days of Christmas" is sure to motivate little learners to create their own simplified class version. Write the numerals from 1 through 12 in a column on a sheet of chart paper. Then help youngsters brainstorm 12 different circus acts and record them on the list. Ask each child to draw a picture of one of the circus acts listed, being sure to include the matching number of characters in his drawing. (If desired, have children work in pairs to illustrate the larger numbers.) Write text for each drawing; then bind the completed pages together into a class book. As you turn to each new page, sing the words to the Christmas tune, turning back to sing the preceding pages each time.

Star of the Circus

"I'm the star of the circus," claims each circus performer in Michael and Mary Beth Sampson's *Star of the Circus* (Henry Holt and Company), until they all realize that it takes an entire team to put on a circus. To show your youngsters what teamwork is all about, invite them to build a human pyramid. In a large open space, position your class as follows: five children sitting in a row on the floor, four children kneeling behind the first row, three children crouched behind the second row, two children standing behind the third row, and a single child standing on a sturdy chair behind the fourth row. (Adjust the number in each row to suit your class size.) When you begin to build the pyramid, have the first child say, "I'm the star of the circus." As each additional child joins the pyramid, have him say, "No, I'm the star of the circus!" When your pyramid is complete, have the class repeat the story's ending by shouting, "We're all stars of the circus!" Be sure to take a Polaroid® photograph of the pyramid so your little circus stars can admire their daring teamwork.

Barnyard Big Top

When Ben's Uncle Julius brings his circus to the farm, everything goes haywire! Youngsters are sure to go hog-wild over the humor of *Barnyard Big Top* by Jill Kastner (Simon & Schuster Books for Young Readers). Ask your little ones what it would be like if their school were turned into a circus. On a sheet of chart paper, write the sentence "One day a circus came to our school." Invite your youngsters to help you write a class story about the events that might take place. Would the principal walk a tightrope over the playground? Would the lions eat up all the food in the cafeteria? Would the bareback riders give the kids rides to the bus stop? Post the story on a wall and let it keep growing as long as children like. Older students may want to illustrate some of the events. At the end of your unit, reread the final story and encourage youngsters to think of an ending.

Circus

Come one, come all to a big top adventure—captured in Lois Ehlert's *Circus* (HarperCollins Juvenile Books). Prepare this art center activity to help little ones imitate Ehlert's unique graphic art style. For each child, cut several stars and a variety of shapes from fluorescent paper. Stock your art center with the cutouts, black construction paper, scissors, scraps of fluorescent paper, and glue. After sharing the story, ask youngsters to examine Ehlert's illustrations again, noting the shapes used to make the circus characters and the border of stars. Then invite each youngster to visit your art center and arrange some fluorescent shapes on a sheet of black paper to make a circus animal or performer. Invite each artist to glue her design to her paper and then add a border of stars. Display these circus creations on a bulletin board with your own Lois Ehlert–style clown (made from fluorescent poster board shapes) and the title "Circus Shapes."

Dinosaurs

Big Creatures, Big Words

Building vocabulary will be a huge success when you describe these larger-than-life reptiles. Begin by writing "Dinosaurs were big" on a sheet of chart paper. Read the sentence to the class; then invite a volunteer to point to the word *big*. Together, brainstorm other words that describe the massive size of most dinosaurs, such as *large, huge, humongous,* and *gigantic*. Label a separate sticky note with each response; then stack the notes over the word *big*. Ask the class to read the sentence aloud using the word on the top sticky note. Then remove the note and read the sentence again with the next word. When all the notes are removed, reread the original sentence.

To extend this activity for older students, invite each child to copy the sentence onto a sheet of chart paper, substituting her favorite adjective for the word *big*. Then have her illustrate her sentence.

Dinosaurs were enormous.

tremendous

fat

D Is for Dinosaur

Watch confusion over the letters *b* and *d* become extinct with this helpful hint. In advance, randomly program each of a class supply of notecards with either a *b* or a *d*. Mark the top of each card with a dot. Write a large *d* on chart paper.

Say the word *dinosaur*. Ask youngsters to identify the letter and sound at the beginning of the word. Then show them the letter on the chart paper. Ask youngsters to imagine that the rounded part of the *d* is a dinosaur's tummy. Explain that since big ol' dinosaurs are always hungry, their tummies are always the first things you see (as you read from left to right). Then transform the letter into a dinosaur as shown. Distribute the index cards, instructing each child to hold her card so that the dot is at the top. Ask her to decide whether she holds a *b* or *d*. Remind her that if it's the letter *d*, as in *dinosaur,* the tummy comes first. To confirm her answer, have each child compare her card to the *d* on the chart.

Hatching Dinos

Your little paleontologists will practice one-to-one correspondence as they hatch these dinosaur eggs. Place a small dinosaur toy or sticker inside each of ten plastic eggs. Explain to your class that like snakes, toads, and chickens, dinosaurs hatched from eggs. Show students the eggs. Ask them to count the eggs and decide how many dinosaurs will hatch from the egg set. Invite student volunteers to open the dinosaur eggs and chorally count the dinosaurs. Did youngsters guess the correct number?

To vary the activity, set out a desired number of dinosaurs from one to ten and then have your little ones put each dinosaur into an egg. Or to reinforce colors, separate the egg halves; then ask youngsters to match the halves and tuck a dinosaur into each egg. The "egg-citing" variations of this activity are endless!

"Sort-a-saurus"

All sorts of fun and learning will happen when youngsters categorize dinosaur-shaped pasta. To prepare, put a desired amount of dinosaur pasta shapes into a resealable plastic bag. Add one-half cup of rubbing alcohol and a few drops of food coloring; then shake the bag until the pasta is the desired color. Prepare three bags of different pasta colors in this manner. Then spread all the pasta out on paper towels to dry. To use, give each child a cup of ten or more pasta dinosaurs in assorted colors. First, ask him to sort the dinosaurs by color. Then continue the fun by having him sort the pasta by dinosaur type or by different dinosaur characteristics, such as leg count.

Sizing Up Dinosaurs

This dinosaur activity will make a *big* difference in youngsters' size-comparison skills. Ask youngsters to bring their labeled toy dinosaurs from home to help create a collection of dinosaurs in many sizes. Select three dinosaurs of different sizes and show youngsters how to sequence them by size. Describe the dinosaurs as *big, bigger,* and *biggest.* Then name each size again, this time having a student volunteer point to the appropriate dinosaur. Return the dinosaurs to the collection; then select three more dinosaurs and ask a student pair to order and name the dinosaurs by size. Continue in this manner until each child has a turn to help sequence a set of dinosaurs. Then, for a "dino-mite" conclusion, show your class pictures of *Brachiosaurus,* the biggest dinosaur, and *Compsognathus,* the smallest dinosaur. Tell students that the largest creature was as long as two school buses while the smallest was only slightly bigger than a chicken!

Big, bigger, biggest!

Dinosaurs

"Me-a-saurus"

Display pictures of dinosaurs in your block center. Point out various features to describe each dinosaur, such as the long tail, small head, and short front legs of an apatosaurus. Then challenge your little ones to build their own dinosaurs using DUPLO® or LEGO® building blocks. When a dinosaur is complete, take an instant photo of it to display in the block center. Name each dinosaur after its designer; then write the name in the space below the photograph.

Charles-a-saurus

Dinosaurs Were Babies, Too!

Invite your little paleontologists to your sand table for a little dinosaur discovery. Purchase small plastic dinosaurs from a toy store. Or cut dinosaurs from thin craft sponge or craft foam. Place each dinosaur in a plastic egg; then bury the eggs in the sand table. Add some shovels to the table. Then invite youngsters to the center for a dinosaur dig. They're sure to dig the "egg-citing" discovery that awaits them!

Reptile Roll

Strengthen your little reptiles' counting skills with the roll of a die. To prepare, cut six notecards in half. Program each card with a dinosaur sticker or stamp; then place the cards in a basket. Put the basket in the math center along with a set of dice. Invite youngsters to roll the dice and count out the corresponding number of dinosaur cards. If desired, have younger children use only one die. Or add a third die and additional dinosaur cards to challenge more advanced students. Youngsters are sure to think this counting activity is "dino-mite"!

Fossil Finds

These dinosaur fossils are sure to leave a lasting impression. Place rolling pins and an assortment of small plastic or rubber dinosaurs in your play dough center. Encourage your little paleontologists to roll out play dough patties. Have them press the dinosaurs firmly into the patties, then remove them to discover the resulting imprints. After making several dinosaur impressions, encourage each fossil finder to match each of his dinosaurs to its fossil print. It's a find of a lifetime!

Prehistoric Estimation

Add some prehistoric splash to your water-table fun with this estimation activity. To prepare, cut islands of various sizes from colored Styrofoam® meat trays. Use a pencil to poke several holes in a few of the islands. Then put the islands, along with a quantity of small plastic dinosaurs, into your water table. Encourage each child to guess how many dinosaurs it will take to sink one of the islands. Then have her add one lovable lizard at a time to the island until it goes under water. Splash!

Dinosaurs

"Count-a-saurus"

Teach the following dinosaur ditty to reinforce counting skills.

(sung to the tune of "Five Little Ducks")

One little dino went out to play,
Out in a muddy swamp one day.
He had such enormous fun.
He called for another dinosaur to come.

Two little dinos…
Three little dinos…
Four little dinos…

Five little dinos went out to play,
Out in a muddy swamp one day.
Then Mama called, "Come down the path!
It's time for you all to take a bubble bath!"

Directional Dinos

Direct your students to better math and language skills with this activity. Use the patterns on page 192 to cut a construction paper dinosaur for each child. Distribute the dinosaurs; then verbally direct the children to place their dinosaurs under their chins, over their heads, behind their backs, etc. Be certain to emphasize each directional concept, such as *under* or *over*. Then have youngsters follow your lead as you silently position your dinosaur between your palms, on top of your knee, or beside your foot. Have students use directional words to describe where their dinosaurs are positioned. Before you know it, your students will have these language concepts *under* control!

40

A Daily Dose of Dinosaur Math

You can count on dinosaurs to make daily math practice fun! Use the patterns on page 192 to cut several dinosaurs of each type from different colors of felt. During each day of your dinosaur unit, use the felt dinosaurs to reinforce a different math skill on your flannelboard. Have students count the dinosaurs as you place them on your flannelboard, then count backwards as you remove each dino. Encourage youngsters to sort the dinosaurs by color or type, then count the dinosaurs in each group. Reinforce ordinal numbers by displaying the dinosaurs in a line and asking the children to identify the dinosaur that is first, second, third, etc. Create a pattern featuring a sequence of colored dinosaurs or different types of dinosaurs; then have students extend the pattern. It's a prehistoric menagerie of math!

Calling All Dinosaurs

Greet each of your little dinos with this reptile roll call.

(sung to the tune of "Where Is Thumbkin?")

Teacher: [Courtney]-a-saurus,
               [Courtney]-a-saurus…
Child: Here I am. Here I am.
Teacher: Hello, little dinosaur!
               Let me hear you stomp and roar!
               Come join in! Come join in!

grrrr

Dinosaur, Dinosaur

Teacher, Teacher, what do you see? You'll see youngsters working on color recognition when you use this variation on the text of Bill Martin, Jr.'s, *Brown Bear, Brown Bear, What Do You See?* (Henry Holt and Company, Inc.). To prepare, use the patterns on page 192 to cut dinosaurs from various colors of construction paper. (If desired, back each cutout with magnetic tape for display on a magnetic surface or with Velcro® for display on a flannelboard.) Then read the Bill Martin, Jr., story to your class. Once students are familiar with the repetitive text, use the dinosaur cutouts to create a "dino-mite" version of the story. Simply display one dinosaur cutout at a time, helping youngsters chime in with the rhyme.

To challenge more advanced students, substitute a set of white dinosaur cutouts labeled with color words.

Red Dino, Red Dino, what do you see? I see an orange dino looking at me.

Dinosaurs

Designer Dinosaurs

Scientists have learned much about dinosaurs from their bones, but no one is really sure what color dinosaurs were. Invite youngsters to take an imaginary trip back in time to discover some dinosaur colors. Have them close their eyes; then describe a dinosaur with colorful stripes, spots, or perhaps even *plaid* skin. Invite some of the children to describe the dinosaurs they see in their imaginations. Afterward, provide youngsters with construction paper copies of the dinosaur pattern on page 193, as well as sticky dots, scissors, rulers, and crayons. Have each child cut out her pattern; then invite her to use the items to decorate her dinosaur as she desires. Display these designer dinosaurs on a bulletin board titled "Just Imagine!"

Yummy Excavation Station

Young explorers will get a taste of what digging for dinosaurs is like at this yummy excavation site. In advance, purchase Gummy dinosaurs, chocolate cookies, one box of instant chocolate pudding for every four students, and enough milk to prepare the pudding. Also, gather a class supply of paper cups and plastic spoons. Then enlist the help of small student groups to prepare the chocolate pudding according to the package directions. Invite each child to mix the pudding with an eggbeater for some extra fine-motor fun. Once the pudding is prepared, have each child place a Gummy dinosaur in the bottom of her cup. Then have her spoon a serving of chocolate-pudding mud over the dinosaur. Give her a cookie to crumble into her cup to create a layer of soil. Then ask her to excavate the dinosaur using a spoon shovel. Once her dinosaur is unearthed, invite the young paleontologist to gobble it up. Now that's a tasty dinosaur dig!

"Color-a-saurus"

Youngsters will exercise their small finger muscles with this color matching center. To prepare, buy a package of large paper clips in assorted colors. Duplicate the dinosaur pattern (page 193) on tagboard colors corresponding to each paper-clip color; then cut out each pattern. Laminate the cutouts for durability. Place the paper clips and dinosaurs in a large resealable plastic bag; then put the bag in a center. To use the center, the child sorts the paper clips by color. Then he slides each paper clip onto the back of a matching dinosaur. Ready? Let's clip some colors!

Dig and Discover

Your pint-sized paleontologists will really dig this puzzling prehistoric adventure. In a tub of sand (or rice), bury pieces of a dinosaur puzzle. Then invite small groups of youngsters to dig into the sand. As each child discovers a puzzle piece, ask him to guess the dinosaur body part. When all the pieces are found, challenge the group to assemble the puzzle without its base—just as paleontologists assemble dinosaur bones into whole skeletons. Piece by piece, youngsters are sure to make a "dino-mite" discovery!

Dino "Trace-O"

Shape up fine-motor skills as youngsters create dinosaur shapes with this neat tracing activity. To prepare, purchase a yard of clear plastic covering from a fabric store (or use a clear plastic tablecloth or a length of laminating film). Spread the clear plastic over a classroom table. Cut the covering slightly smaller than the tabletop; then tape three edges to the table. Collect dry erase markers, chalk erasers, and a few simple dinosaur illustrations (such as the dinosaur pattern on page 193). If desired, also provide word cards with dinosaur names printed on them. Slide the dinosaur pictures and cards under the clear covering.

A child at this center uses dry erase markers to trace a dinosaur picture or name onto the clear plastic. When she is done, she can erase her dinosaur drawing with an eraser. If the child doesn't want to part with her dinosaur, have her trace it onto a sheet of paper. Then encourage her to take her reptile relic home.

brontosaurus

Dinosaurs

Dino Limbo

Watch your youngsters move and groove to the Dino Limbo! Have your little ones pretend to be dinosaurs making their way through a thick forest. Using a long dowel or a broom handle as a limbo stick, invite your dinosaurs to perform the following actions as they move under the limbo stick: crawl on all fours, slither on their stomachs and backs, and roll like a log. For an additional challenge, vary the height of the stick and ask your dinos to go under the stick T-rex style—on their hind legs. How low can your dinos go?

Dino Ditty

Your dinos will delight in this dinosaur ditty. It's "dino-mite"!

Dinosaur, dinosaur, turn around.
Dinosaur, dinosaur, jump up and down.
Dinosaur, dinosaur, bend your knee.
Dinosaur, dinosaur, throw a kiss to me.
Dinosaur, dinosaur, touch your toes.
Dinosaur, dinosaur, wrinkle your nose.
Dinosaur, dinosaur, hop around.
Dinosaur, dinosaur, sit on the ground.

Dino Dig

Give your little paleontologists an activity they will definitely dig! Collect some chicken and beef bones from your local butcher; then boil the bones until the meat is off. Gather a large, white, plastic egg for each child; then put a dinosaur figure or sticker inside each egg. Hide the bones and eggs in your outdoor sandbox. Then send your paleontologists to the sandbox equipped with sand shovels to make a "dino-riffic" find of a lifetime!

Roam on the Range

Your little ones will have a rip-roarin' time as they roam through this recreational realm! Use the playground equipment and classroom props listed below to make a challenging outdoor course. When the route is ready, lead your roving reptiles through the following obstacles:

Obstacles:
leap over stepping-stones
crawl through a cave
climb under thick vines
jump over a river
climb up and down a mountain
walk on a log over water

Materials needed:
wooden blocks or cardboard bricks
open-ended appliance box or small table
swings
two parallel jump ropes
slide
balance beam

Cave Walk

Create a deep, dark cave that only the bravest dinosaurs will enter! Drape dark fabric across the openings of an indoor play tunnel, and designate the tunnel as a dinosaur cave. Then make a cave path by placing jump ropes end-to-end on the floor leading up to the cave. Ask a few youngsters to stand with space in between each other alongside the ropes. Have these children use two hands to hold plastic hoops at their sides.

Then have the remaining children form a line. Encourage them to walk on the ropes and through each hoop. If they fall off a rope or touch the side of a hoop, they run to the end of the line and try again to reach the cave. Don't forget to give the hoop holders a chance to enter the cave, too…if they dare!

Dinosaurs

Dino Land

Ingredients:
1 graham cracker per child
soft cream cheese
green food coloring
3 Gummy dinosaurs per child

Utensils and Supplies:
1 plastic knife (or craft stick) per child
napkins
spoon

Teacher Preparation:
Tint cream cheese with green food coloring. Arrange the ingredients and utensils near the step-by-step direction cards.

What to Do When the Snack Is Through

Count on dinosaurs for some "tremenda-saurus" sorting practice! Encourage your little dinosaur lovers to sort the leftover Gummy dinosaurs by color and then by type. Have youngsters count the number of dinosaurs in each group. Can your students name the group with the most dinosaurs? The fewest dinosaurs? There's much fun in store with "dino-sorts"!

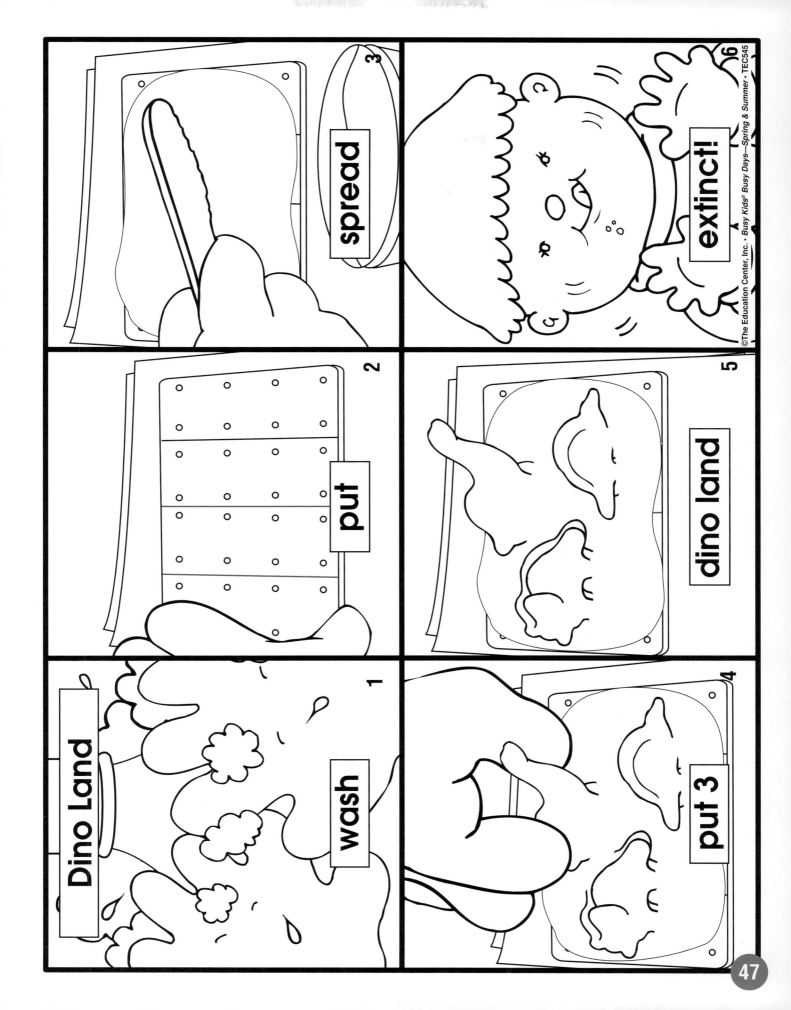

spread

3

extinct!

6

put

2

dino land

5

Dino Land

wash

1

put 3

4

Dinosaurs

Oh, yes, I know Stegosaurus...

Do You Know Your Dinosaurs?

(sung to the tune of "Muffin Man")

Oh, do you know [Triceratops],
[Triceratops], [Triceratops]?
Oh, do you know [Triceratops],
[With three horns on his head]?

Oh, yes, I know [Triceratops],
[Triceratops], [Triceratops].
Oh, yes, I know [Triceratops],
[With three horns on his head].

Repeat the song, replacing the dinosaur name and the last line of each verse with one of the following:

Apatosaurus...His neck is very long.
Stegosaurus...With plates upon his back.
The fierce T-Rex...The King of Dinosaurs.

A Dino's Day

Fuel your youngsters' imaginations with this action rhyme and the accompanying movements.

Welcome to a dino's day.
Let's act like them in *every* way!

Roar like a dinosaur.   *Roar.*
Run for some dino fun.   *Run in place.*
Fly in the dino sky.   *Spread arms and "fly."*
Eat up a dino treat.   *Pretend to eat.*
Sit for a dino bit.   *Sit on the floor.*

That was fun,
You did your best.
Now, it's time for a dino rest.   *Rest head on folded hands.*

Prehistoric Prints

Teach youngsters this dinosaur rhyme; then invite them to make fossil imprints by pressing small plastic dinosaurs into play dough.

When dinosaurs walked upon this land
Millions of years ago,
They left footprints in clay and sand
Wherever they happened to go.

Time has passed by. Those prints are dry
And hardened just like stone.
Today these fossils help us learn
Where dinosaurs used to roam.

Dinosaur, Dinosaur

Get your little reptiles up and movin' to this adaptation of the popular "Teddy Bear, Teddy Bear" chant.

Dinosaur, Dinosaur,
Stamp your feet.   *Stamp feet.*
Dinosaur, Dinosaur,
Show your teeth.   *Show teeth.*

Dinosaur, Dinosaur,
Swing your tail.   *Sway arm behind back.*
Dinosaur, Dinosaur,
Touch your scales.   *Touch belly.*

Dinosaur, Dinosaur,
Show your claws.   *Bend fingers like claws.*
Dinosaur, Dinosaur,
Open your jaws.   *Open mouth.*

Dinosaur, Dinosaur,
Give a roar.   *Roar.*
Dinosaur, Dinosaur,
Sit on the floor.   *Sit down.*

49

Dinosaurs

Dinosaurs, Dinosaurs

Your little dinosaur lovers are sure to dig Byron Barton's simple description of our prehistoric pals in *Dinosaurs, Dinosaurs* (HarperTrophy). After sharing the story, divide a sheet of chart paper into two columns with these headings: "Some dinosaurs had…" and "Some dinosaurs were…" Brainstorm together words from the book to describe physical characteristics of some dinosaurs, such as horns or spikes. List these words in column one. In column two, list words from the story that describe how the dinosaurs were, such as fierce or hungry. When possible, add simple illustrations to help prereaders remember the words. Next, teach the children the following chant. Encourage them to tap their knees with their hands to a steady beat. Pause during the last line of each verse and ask a student volunteer to insert a word from the corresponding column on the chart.

○	○
Some dinosaurs had…	Some dinosaurs were…
horns	fierce
spikes	scared
clubs on their tails	hungry
armored plates	tired
sharp claws	

This is how the dinosaurs looked, dinosaurs looked, dinosaurs looked.
This is how the dinosaurs looked.
They had…[horns].

This is how the dinosaurs were, dinosaurs were, dinosaurs were.
This is how the dinosaurs were.
They were…[fierce].

Saturday Night at the Dinosaur Stomp

"Slick back your scales and get ready to romp…." It's *Saturday Night at the Dinosaur Stomp* by Carol Diggory Shields (Candlewick Press). Introduce your youngsters to many different kinds of dancing dinosaurs in this tale of a Jurassic boogie bash. Then invite your little dinosaur dancers to join you in this chant at your own dinosaur stomp.

Dinosaur Stomp

Boomalacka! Boomalacka!   *Slap hands on legs three times.*
Whack! Whack! Whack!   *Wiggle body down to the floor.*
[Boogie on down], dinosaurs.
Don't hold back!

Create additional verses by inserting these words and actions:
Stomp your feet….   *Stomp feet.*
Shake your scales….   *Shake all over.*
Twist your tails….   *Hold arm behind back and twist wrist.*
Wiggle your claws….   *Wiggle fingers.*

Can I Have a Stegosaurus, Mom? Can I? Please!?

An imaginative little boy asks, *Can I Have a Stegosaurus, Mom? Can I? Please!?* in this tale by Lois G. Grambling (Troll Associates, Inc.). A surprise ending develops as a cracking dinosaur egg hatches and the little boy comes back to his mom with another question: "Can I have a Tyrannosaurus Rex, Mom...Can I? PLEASE!?" Use this ending to spark your youngsters' imaginations about having a prehistoric pet of their own. Invite youngsters to close their eyes and imagine themselves with a giant T-rex. After giving little ones a minute to think, invite each child to complete this sentence: "If I had a T-rex, Mom, I would..." Write down his response on a sheet of paper; then encourage him to illustrate his sentence. Bind the drawings together into a class book. Have youngsters take turns taking this book home to show their moms, who are sure to be delighted that dinosaurs are extinct!

If I had a T-rex, Mom,
I would let him sleep in my bed.

My Dinosaur

It's a dream come true in Mark Alan Weatherby's *My Dinosaur* (Scholastic Trade Books) as a little girl has a moonlit adventure with her prehistoric pet. To follow up this dreamy story, make a read-along tape of the story to put in your listening center. Record yourself reading the book in your best dreamy voice. If desired, whistle when the text says the girl whistled; slurp when it says they drank at the river; and sing the goodnight song to the tune of "Happy Birthday to You" (say the last line). At the beginning of the tape, instruct youngsters to turn the page when they hear the sound of a bell (or another chosen signal). Once you're done recording, play the tape for the class as you turn the pages of the book. If necessary, remind youngsters to turn the pages at the sound of the bell. Place the tape and a copy of the book in your listening center for your children to enjoy independently. Sweet dreams!

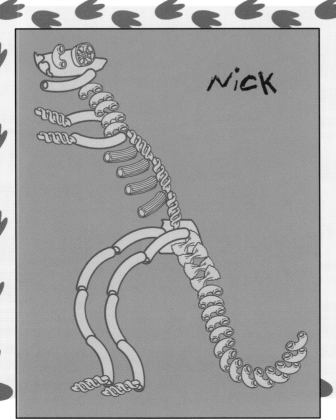

Big Old Bones: A Dinosaur Tale

Your little ones are certain to know more about dinosaurs than one very puzzled Professor Potts in *Big Old Bones: A Dinosaur Tale* by Carol Carrick (Clarion Books). Your dinosaur experts will be anxious to correct the professor as he makes some big dino blunders. Be sure to call their attention to the professor's young assistant, who is always one step ahead of Potts. After sharing this dino delight, have your little ones create dinosaur skeletons of their own. To prepare, gather some pictures of dinosaur skeletons to place in your art center. Add glue, dark construction paper, and an assortment of dried pasta. Tell your pint-sized paleontologists that you have unearthed these "bones" and need their help in piecing them together to make a dinosaur. For the child who has trouble getting started, lightly sketch a simple dinosaur body and have him glue the bones to the sketch. Encourage youngsters to be as imaginative as Professor Potts!

Rain

Counting on Rain

Reinforce number skills right down to the last drop of this rain activity. To prepare, put eyedroppers, blue-tinted water, permanent markers, white construction paper, and a set of magnetic numerals in your discovery center. To practice making raindrops, invite each child to use an eyedropper to squeeze blue water droplets onto a sheet of paper. Encourage him to drop the rain from various heights above his paper to create raindrops of different sizes. Then help him fold another sheet of paper twice to create four equal sections. Have him unfold his paper; then ask him to copy a different numeral on each section, using the magnetic numerals as references. Direct the child to squeeze the corresponding number of raindrops onto each section.

One raindrop, two raindrops,…

A Shapely Rainbow

Chase away rainy day blues with this color and shape review. To begin, draw a large outline of a rainbow on white bulletin board paper. Pencil in the appropriate color words from top to bottom—red, orange, yellow, green, blue, purple. Make several tagboard tracers for each of six shapes, such as circles, squares, triangles, rectangles, ovals, and hearts. Then gather construction paper in the rainbow colors. Divide your class into six groups. Assign each group a different color and shape. Ask each group member to trace her assigned shape several times onto the appropriate paper color. Have her cut out each shape and then glue it onto the corresponding section of the rainbow. Wow! A colorful rainbow takes shape!

Brainstorm Rainstorm

With this rhyming "brainstorm," it'll be raining cats and dogs...and bats and hogs...and hats and logs! Cut out a quantity of raindrops from light blue construction paper. Program each of several raindrops with a word family (rime), such as *at, ed, ig, op,* or *ug.* Open a large umbrella; then tape one programmed raindrop onto the umbrella. Help youngsters pronounce the word ending. Then challenge them to brainstorm words with the same ending. Label a separate raindrop with each student response; then tape it to the umbrella. On subsequent days, ask students to brainstorm words belonging to the other word families. Keep the umbrella on display in your writing center to inspire a downpour of creativity.

Somewhere Over the Rainbow

Look to this rainbow activity to give youngsters valuable language skills practice. Place the rainbow made in "A Shapely Rainbow" (page 52) in an open area of your room; then seat a small group of children in a half circle around it. Give each child a few gold-wrapped chocolate coins. Then sing this tune, filling in the blank with a positional word or phrase, such as *over, on top of, next to, under,* or *behind.* Instruct youngsters to place a gold coin as directed each time you sing the song. After several rounds, invite each of your lucky leprechauns to retrieve his gold coins for a tasty treat!

(sung to the tune of "Somewhere Over the Rainbow")
Somewhere [over] the rainbow,
I ask you
To place your coin of gold,
So good luck will come to you!

Pitter-Patter Patterning

Shower little ones with some pitter-patter patterning in this tasty raindrop activity. In advance, buy a class supply of lollipops in a variety of colors, making sure you have at least four of each color. Cut out a class supply (plus a few extras) of construction paper raindrops, sizing each one to cover a lollipop; then tape a lollipop to each cutout. Give each child a raindrop lollipop. Then arrange seven youngsters in a row in front of the group, creating an ABAB pattern with their lollipop colors. Then sing this song, naming the two lollipop colors in the appropriate lines. Invite youngsters to hold up their raindrop lollipops when their color is sung in the fourth line. Repeat the activity a few times with different children and different lollipop color patterns; then ask students to create their own ABAB patterns. And when you're all done singing and patterning, invite each child to sample her tasty raindrop.

(sung to the tune of "If All the Raindrops")

If all the raindrops were [blue] and [purple] lollipops,
Oh, what a rain it would be!
Standing in line with my hands help up high,
[Blue, purple, blue, purple, blue, purple, blue.]
If all the raindrops were [blue] and [purple] lollipops,
Oh, what a rain it would be!

Rain

Rain Gear

Gear up for wet weather by stocking your dramatic-play center with rainy-day attire. In advance, ask parents to send in rain gear, such as galoshes, ponchos, boots, rain hats, and slickers. (You may want to discourage parents from sending in umbrellas, since they can be a bit hazardous during free play.) Encourage parents to label articles of clothing with their children's names. Add the items to your dramatic-play center. Laminate puddles cut from blue construction paper; then tape them to the floor for "splashing." Ask youngsters to name the various articles of clothing as they parade around in their puddle-stompin' gear.

It's raining balloons!   *Kenny*

Cloudy With a Chance of "Brainstorms"

The forecast for this idea calls for a flood of imagination! To prepare, place a bag of colored cotton balls, glue, crayons, and white construction paper in your art center. Demonstrate for students how to stretch a cotton ball to create a cloud. Then have each child stretch and glue wispy clusters of cotton-ball clouds onto a sheet of white construction paper. After students create their clouds, encourage them to draw imaginative items falling from the clouds. Ask each youngster to describe his drawing to you; then record his descriptions on his paper. Be sure to batten down the hatches for the brainstorms headed your way!

Counting in the Rain

Give little fingers a workout counting raindrops. Supply a center with eyedroppers, clear plastic cups, and numerals cut from craft foam. Partially fill some of the cups with blue-tinted water. Demonstrate for students how to use an eyedropper to transfer water from a water-filled cup to an empty one. Allow students at this center to experiment and practice using their eyedroppers. Then have each child pour all his water back into one cup. Instruct him to select a numeral from the basket; then have him drop the corresponding number of raindrops into his empty cup. Encourage him to continue in this manner until he's enjoyed the last drop!

Rain Check

Take advantage of a rainy day by checking out some raindrops. When the forecast calls for rain, set up your discovery center with a cup, blue food coloring, an eyedropper, a spoon, toothpicks, and waxed paper. Invite small groups to observe single raindrops as they travel down a classroom windowpane and collide with other drops. Then send a child out to collect some rainwater in the cup. Mix blue food coloring into the rainwater to make it more visible. Then provide each child with a toothpick and a piece of waxed paper. Using the eyedropper, put a few drops of rainwater on each child's waxed paper. Encourage each child to explore the drops with his toothpick. Can he make the drops wiggle or break into smaller drops? Can he combine all the drops into one large raindrop? The forecast for this activity is clear—wet and wild!

From Drizzle to Downpour

Shower your students with some rainy-day vocabulary at your water table. To prepare, remove the lids from three whipped-topping containers; then punch holes in the bottom of each container. Make tiny holes in the first container, medium-sized holes in the second, and large holes in the last container. Place the containers in your water table. Introduce your youngsters to some words that describe rain, such as *sprinkle, drizzle, shower,* or *downpour.* Then encourage them to visit your water table for a demonstration. Invite children to fill the different containers with water, hold them above the water table, and then determine what kind of rain results from each one. Pitter-patter. Drip-drop. Splish-splash!

Rain

Rain—Friend or Foe?

Chase away the rainy-day blues with this language activity that will have everyone thinking happy thoughts about rain. Inflate a large blue balloon; then introduce it to the class as a raindrop. Have your youngsters sit in a circle, then pass the raindrop as you repeatedly sing the traditional song "Rain, Rain, Go Away." Insert each child's name in the song as he holds the balloon.

Next, ask youngsters if they enjoy the rain or wish it would go away. Discuss the activities they enjoy doing inside and outside on a rainy day. Then ask students to think about the good things rain provides for people and the earth. Pass the balloon raindrop around again. As each child holds the balloon, encourage him to share one good thing about the rain.

Note: Balloons can be a choking hazard for small children. Provide close supervision.

Shower Power

Use seedlings to demonstrate the importance of rain. Purchase two small seedlings from a nursery. Tape a blue paper raindrop to one seedling's pot. Explain to your youngsters that this plant will be given water from a watering can, to simulate rain. Tape a blue raindrop with a black slash mark through it on the second seedling's pot. Explain that this plant will not be given water, to simulate dry weather. Provide a watering can for a volunteer to water the first plant, and then set both seedlings on a windowsill. Ask your youngsters to predict what will happen after a few days. Each day for several days, observe the plants and the changes that are taking place. Water the first plant daily. After several days it will be obvious that rain showers make happy flowers! Extend the lesson by giving a dose of water to the second plant and observing its improvement.

The Colors of the Rainbow

Find a lesson on colors when you look over this rainbow! In advance cut three-foot streamers from red, orange, yellow, green, blue, and purple crepe paper. Write the corresponding color words on large index cards. Give each child one streamer and have him identify the color. Once everyone has a streamer, display one index card and announce the color word. Have all the children with streamers of that color gather together in a designated spot. Repeat this process with the other colors until all youngsters have been grouped. Then put on some instrumental music, and invite all the colors of the rainbow to move freely around your classroom.

Rainmaker

Make it rain in the classroom with this easy science demonstration. Seat children in a semicircle, so they can watch the rainstorm from a safe distance. Fill a Crock-Pot® with water; then set it on a small table in front of your group. Plug in the Crock-Pot® and boil the water. Fill an aluminum pie plate with ice cubes and hold it over the steaming water. Observe together as the steam touches the cold pie plate, condenses into water drops, and then falls down like rain. It's a drip-drop drama!

Weather Watch

The forecast for this weather activity is developing skills with observation, recording data, and comparing data! Create a monthly weather graph by dividing a sheet of chart paper into three columns labeled "Sunny," "Rainy," and "Cloudy." Draw a corresponding symbol next to each label. Select one child each day to be the weather watcher; then sing the following weather song. Have the weather watcher look out the window, give a weather report, and then draw an "x" in the column that best represents the weather for the day. At the end of the month, count and compare the number of sunny, cloudy, and rainy days.

(sung to the tune of "Where Is Thumbkin?")
Weather watcher,
Weather watcher,
Look outside,
Look outside,
Tell us what the weather's like,
Tell us what the weather's like,
Sun, rain, clouds?
Sun, rain, clouds?

Rain

Unique Umbrellas

Shower your youngsters with fine-motor fun when they make these lacing umbrellas. For each child, enlarge and duplicate the umbrella pattern on page 194 onto tagboard; then cut a class supply of 40-inch yarn lengths. Working with one small group at a time, have each child cut out a pattern; then help her punch holes as indicated on her cutout. Invite her to decorate her cutout with markers. Then help her thread one end of her yarn through the top center hole and tie it in place. Have her lace her cutout as shown; then help her knot the loose end of her yarn near the top hole (on the back side) and trim off any extra length. Now her unique umbrella is ready for some singing in the rain!

Down the Spout

Use this scoop-and-pour activity to help little ones explore how rainwater flows down a spout. To prepare, purchase a straight length and a corner piece of PVC pipe from your local hardware store. Connect the pieces together to re-semble a downspout; then place the downspout on a section of the floor covered with a beach towel. Provide a bucket half-filled with water, as well as a large scoop or measuring cup. Ask each child who visits this center to hold the pipe inside the bucket, with the corner piece at the bottom. Instruct him to scoop water from the bucket, and then pour it into the top of the downspout. Whoosh! Down came the rain….

Flood Warning!

Youngsters will be flooding your fine-motor center to try out this activity! To prepare, gather several empty individual-sized milk cartons; then cut off the top of each carton. Cover the carton with white Con-Tact® paper and then use permanent markers to make the carton resemble a house. Put each milk-carton house in a dishpan. Then provide a bucket of water, scoops, sand sieves, and eyedroppers.

At this center, a child holds a sieve over his milk-carton house. He scoops some water from the bucket, then pours the water into his sieve to create a downpour over his house. When his milk-carton house is flooded with water, challenge him to embark on a rescue mission. Have him remove the water from the house with an eyedropper. After all the water has been returned to the bucket, invite the child to congratulate himself on his heroic efforts.

Rainbows Filtering Through

The forecast for this paint-and-peel activity is a downpour of enthusiasm, followed by rainbows galore! Cut a supply of coffee filters in half; then put

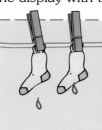

them on a table along with watercolor paints, paintbrushes, containers of water, and large sheets of white construction paper. Direct each youngster to place a coffee-filter half on a sheet of paper. Have him paint the coffee filter in rainbow colors; then help him carefully peel it off his paper to reveal a colorful rainbow. Set the filter aside to dry. Encourage each child to paint several coffee-filter halves in the same manner, placing each one on a different section of his paper. After all the rainbow art dries, display each child's rainbow-filled paper on a bulletin board. Border the display with the painted coffee filters.

Left Out in the Rain

Oops! The laundry was left out in the rain and now the clothes need wringing out! Enlist the help of your youngsters to squeeze the water out of the dripping laundry with this idea. First, hang a clothesline in an open area of your classroom. Lay a large beach towel on the floor under the clothesline. Hang a few articles of doll or infant clothing on the line with clothespins. Then place water-filled spray bottles on the towel along with an empty bucket. Invite small groups of children to create a rain shower by lightly spraying water onto the clothes. When the clothes begin to drip with water, have youngsters stop the rainstorm. Ask each child to remove one item at a time from the line. Have her wring the excess water from the item into the bucket; then invite her to clip the clothes back on the line to dry. Now let's hope for sunshine!

Rain

Raindrop Balloons

Got the rainy-day blues? Give spirits a lift with raindrop balloons! In advance, inflate a blue balloon for each child plus some extras (in case some pop!). Give a balloon to each child; then ask the children to pretend they are holding giant raindrops. Say, "It's raining!" Then have the children tap the balloons up into the air, and watch them rain down from the sky. Repeat the rain shower, challenging youngsters to keep the raindrops from touching the ground. Instruct little ones to use their heads, elbows, knees, or feet to keep the balloons aloft. Save the raindrops for more rainy-day fun. Bet your youngsters won't want this rain to go away!

Note: Balloons can be a choking hazard for small children. Provide close supervision.

Under an Umbrella

Caught in the rain? How about a giant umbrella to keep your entire class dry? Pretend a parachute or large sheet is a giant umbrella. Have everyone grab hold of the umbrella and say the following chant:

Umbrella up! Umbrella down!
Umbrella, umbrella, round and round.

Raise parachute up; pull parachute down.
Walk in a circle.

Umbrella in! Umbrella out!
Umbrella, umbrella, all about.

Move toward the center; return.
Walk in a circle.

Umbrella high! Umbrella low!
Umbrella, umbrella, here we go.

Raise parachute high; lower it to the ground.
Walk in a circle.

Umbrella fast! Umbrella slow!
Umbrella, umbrella, blow, blow, blow!

Circle quickly; circle slowly.
Shake parachute.

Where is the rain? It's gone away!
We'll fold you up for another day.

Look up at sky.
Gather parachute and fold.

Raindrop Workout

Use the balloons from "Raindrop Balloons" on page 60 to give little muscles a workout. Provide a balloon for each child. Ask youngsters to gently squeeze the balloons between their knees. Challenge little ones to walk or jump without letting the balloons fall. Next, help each child position his balloon between his forearms. Can the youngsters twist their arms from side to side? Can they lift the balloons with their elbows to their ears and back down again? To close the activity and loosen up tight muscles, dance with the raindrop balloons to a recording of "Singin' in the Rain."

Puddle Jumping

Grab your galoshes and get ready for some puddle jumping! Spread a class supply of plastic hoops, plus one for yourself, on the floor. Make certain there is adequate space between the hoops. Encourage each child to select a hoop and pretend it is a big puddle of rainwater. Now go puddle jumping! Ask youngsters to follow along as you demonstrate how to tiptoe, hop, and skip around the outside of your puddle. Now jump right in, first with one foot, then with two feet. Stomp and splash away!

Rainmakers

Create a rainstorm that will leave a rainbow of smiles behind. First, have your youngsters make rainmakers. To make one, fold and crease a paper plate in half. Use crayons or markers to color a rainbow on one half of the folded plate, then color raindrops on the flip side. Leaving a small opening at the top, staple the sides of the plate together, colored sides out. Pour a handful of beans through the opening; then staple it shut. To simulate a rainstorm, have students hold their rainmakers with the raindrops facing out. Give your little ones the following verbal cues; then lead them in the corresponding movements. Don't forget your umbrella!

Teacher Says:

I hear a pitter-patter. The rain is coming near.	*Shake rainmaker slowly.*
Oh, no! It's really pouring. Now the storm is here!	*Dance; shake rainmaker quickly.*
The rain is letting up now, and going on its way.	*Shake rainmaker slowly.*
Here comes a big, bright rainbow to end this rainy day.	*Turn plate to show rainbow; hold it still.*

Rain

Rainbow Cookie

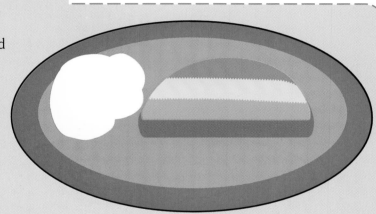

Ingredients:
1 Stella D'oro® Anisette Sponge® cookie per child
whipped topping
food coloring
1 1/2 cups milk

Utensils and Supplies:
1 small paper plate per child
3 plastic bowls
new, thin paintbrushes
spoon

Teacher Preparation:
   Pour a half cup of milk into each of three plastic
bowls. Use food coloring to tint one bowl of milk red,
one yellow, and one green. Put a new, thin paintbrush
in each container of milk. Arrange the ingredients and
utensils near the step-by-step direction cards.

What to Do When
the Snack Is Through
   Give each youngster a dollop of whipped topping
on a paper plate and invite him to mix a drop of food
coloring into the topping with his fingers. Encourage
him to add a drop of a different color to the whipped
topping and mix it in. What new color has he created?
When he is through experimenting with the colors,
invite him to lick his fingers clean!

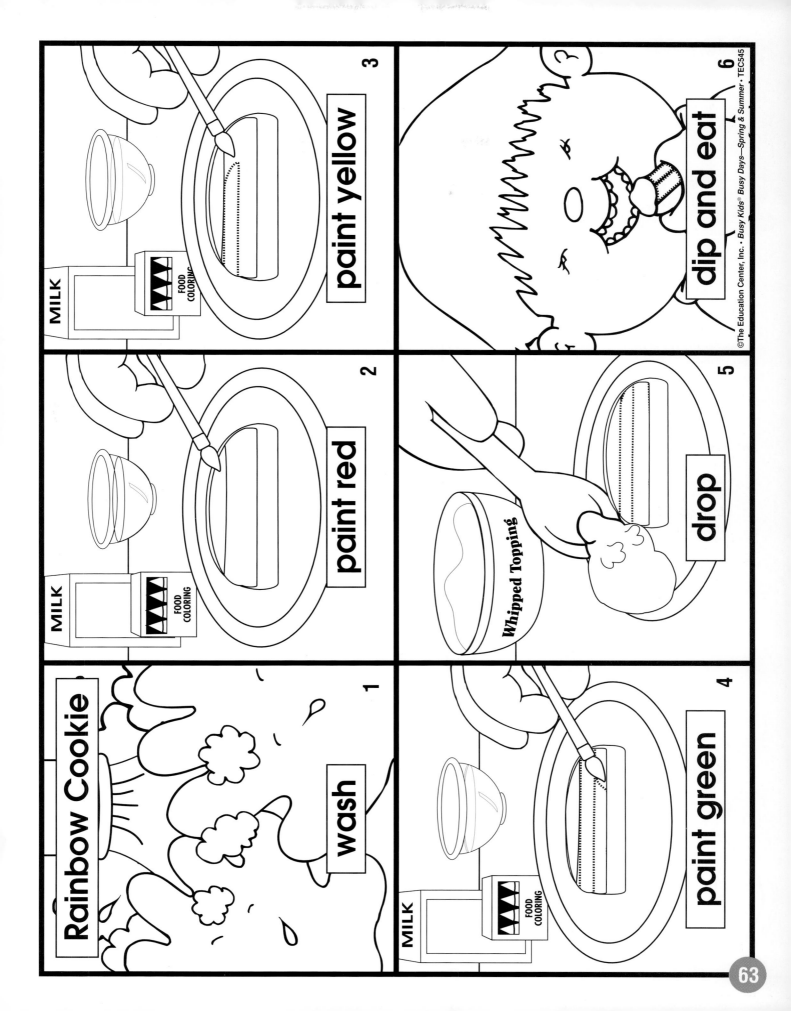

Rainbow Cookie

1 wash

2 paint red

3 paint yellow

4 paint green

5 drop

Whipped Topping

6 dip and eat

MILK

FOOD COLORING

Rain

Keepin' Away Those Rainy Day Blues

On a rainy day, sing this song to your youngsters; then ask them to brainstorm suggestions for keeping away the rainy day blues. Choose a few ideas from their list that are feasible for your classroom. Then take a vote on their favorite classroom blues buster and invite them to enjoy that activity.

(sung to the tune of "Rain, Rain, Go Away")

Rain, rain,
Here to stay,
How could we have fun today?
Oh, what could we do
To keep away the blues?

- read books
- play with play dough
- paint pictures
- watch a video
- eat cookies

Rain From the Clouds

Highlight three kinds of rainstorms with this participatory song. During the first verse, invite youngsters to lightly tap their fingertips on a tabletop to represent a drizzle. Then have them tap their fingers increasingly harder for each additional verse as the rain changes from a drizzle into a downpour.

(sung to the tune of "The Wheels on the Bus")

The rain from the sky goes pit-pit-patter,
Pit-pit-patter, pit-pit-patter.
The rain from the sky goes pit-pit-patter,
As it drizzles down.

The rain from the sky goes drip-drip-drop,
Drip-drip-drop, drip-drip-drop.
The rain from the sky goes drip-drip-drop,
As it showers down.

The rain from the sky goes splish-splish-splash,
Splish-splish-splash, splish-splish-splash.
The rain from the sky goes splish-splish-splash,
As it pours on down!

Walking in the Rain

Youngsters will have a wet and wild time as they splash through this song. Create a path of carpet-square puddles. (Or use laminated construction paper puddle cutouts.) Then invite your little puddle jumpers to splash from one puddle to the next as they sing along.

*(sung to the tune of
"In the Merry, Merry Month of May")*

I was walking in the rain one day.
There were water puddles in the way.
So I splished and then I splashed,
As I walked along the path.
Walking in the rain one day!

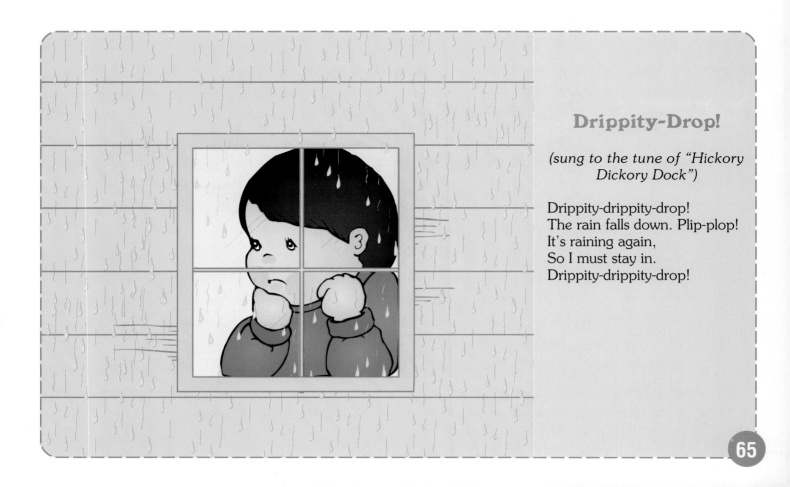

Drippity-Drop!

(sung to the tune of "Hickory Dickory Dock")

Drippity-drippity-drop!
The rain falls down. Plip-plop!
It's raining again,
So I must stay in.
Drippity-drippity-drop!

Rain

In the Rain With Baby Duck

Have you ever heard of a duck that hates the rain? Well, meet Baby Duck of *In the Rain With Baby Duck* by Amy Hest (Candlewick Press). Baby Duck pouts in the rain, until Grampa comes to the rescue with a bright red umbrella and matching boots. After sharing this delightful story, invite your little ones to make their very own Baby Ducks. To prepare, cut enough small paper plates in half so each child will have one half. Scallop the straight edge of each plate half to resemble an umbrella. For each child, precut a 4-inch circle, a 2½-inch circle, and two 2-inch triangles from yellow construction paper. Also precut a 2-inch diamond from orange construction paper, folding it in half to create a beak shape.

To make Baby Duck, glue a large and small circle to a construction paper background as shown. Glue the beak and two wiggle eyes to the head. Use a red marker to add Baby Duck's boots. To make the umbrella, paint the paper plate half with red paint (or a creative watercolor design). Once the paint is dry, staple a pipe cleaner handle to the umbrella and then glue the umbrella top to the top of the paper. To make Baby Duck look like she is holding the umbrella, glue two yellow triangle wings to the sides of Baby Duck's body and then slide the umbrella "handle" under one of them. Finish the project by using a blue marker to add a little downpour over Baby Duck…who *used to* hate the rain.

Rabbits and Raindrops

Rabbits and Raindrops by Jim Arnosky (The Putnam Publishing Group) is the story of five baby rabbits and their first rain. After sharing this inviting story, encourage your little ones to hold up five fingers and count down with you as you sing the following song.

(sung to the tune of "Five Little Ducks Went Out to Play")

Five baby rabbits went out to play	*Hold up five fingers.*
In the green grass on a sunny day.	*Make a round sun using arms.*
But when the rain began to fall,	*Wiggle fingers downward.*
Under the hedge one rabbit crawled.	*Slide one hand under the other.*
Four baby rabbits…	*Hold up four fingers.*
Three baby rabbits…	*Hold up three fingers.*
Two baby rabbits…	*Hold up two fingers.*
One baby rabbit…	*Hold up one finger.*
No baby rabbits went out to play	*Make a zero with fingers.*
In the green grass on that rainy day.	*Wiggle fingers downward.*
Suddenly the rain did stop,	*Hold palms up and look up.*
So out in the sun five rabbits did hop.	*Hop like rabbits.*

April Showers

"Ladies and gentlemen. Children, too. We've just GOT to do a dance for you." Share *April Showers* by George Shannon (Greenwillow Books) and watch five dancing frogs leap, twirl, and shimmy in the rain. Then do some fancy footwork of your own to the following tune—in rain or shine.

(sung to the tune of "The Hokey-Pokey")

We're gonna [tiptoe-twirl].
We're gonna [tiptoe-twirl].
We're gonna [tiptoe-twirl]
On a rainy, rainy day.
We'll shimmy, shimmy, shimmy,
And we'll turn ourselves around,
All on a rainy day.

Substitute these other dance steps from the story or make up your own:
    step-back-hop
    kick-turn-spin
    dance like fools

Rain

Rain, rain, everywhere! After sharing Robert Kalan's *Rain* (Mulberry Books), let it rain all over your little puddle jumpers as they make their own crayon-resist rain pictures. Gather white paper, crayons, and blue watercolors. Have each child draw a picture of herself wearing a raincoat and boots and carrying an umbrella. (Remind her to push down hard on her crayon while drawing and to color in any shapes she makes.) Have her use a white crayon to add raindrops; then have her paint the entire surface of the paper with watercolors. Who can resist splashin' in the rain?

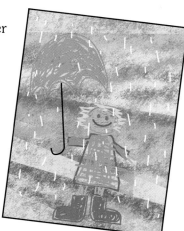

Mushroom in the Rain

How does one mushroom shelter several animals from the rain? Find out in the Russian tale of *Mushroom in the Rain* (Aladdin Paperbacks) by Mirra Ginsburg. Then invite your youngsters to act out this delightful story. Name six student volunteers as different animals from the story. Have remaining students hold the perimeter of a bedsheet to represent the mushroom. If possible, play a tape recording of rain sounds. As each character approaches the mushroom looking for shelter from the rain, he asks, "Is there room enough for me?" Then the youngsters holding the sheet raise it over their heads to gather air resembling a large mushroom. The first character sits under the mushroom, and then the children lower the sheet to the floor over the character. (For a youngster who may be frightened under the sheet, have another adult sit under the sheet with her.) Continue in this manner, with each additional character joining the others under the mushroom. When the fox asks, "Is there room enough for me?" have the other children say, "No!" and shoo the fox away. Act out the story several times to give all your children a turn to hide under the mushroom in the rain.

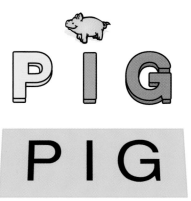

Letters Down on the Farm

Here's a "moo-velous" way for youngsters to practice letter matching and letter sounds. Place some plastic farm animals in a center. Write the name of each animal on a separate sentence strip; then laminate the strips for durability. Put the word strips, magnetic letters, and a magnetic board in the center. To use, a child matches an animal to its corresponding word strip. (Encourage him to use his knowledge of beginning sounds to make each match.) He places the strip on the magnetic board. Then he matches the magnetic letters to the letters on the strip to spell the animal's name.

As a variation for older students, omit the final consonant on each sentence strip label. Challenge children to find the magnetic letter that completes each animal name.

My Teacher Had a Farm

On this farm, you'll hear letter sounds instead of animal sounds! Copy this adapted version of "Old MacDonald Had a Farm" onto chart paper, inserting your name and gender where indicated. Then laminate the chart. Fill in the blank for the animal name with any farm animal; then fill in the remaining blanks with the beginning consonant sound for that animal name. Sing the song with youngsters, emphasizing the beginning consonant sound. Then erase the animal name and letters, replace them with another set, and sing the song again.

As a variation for kindergartners, fill in animal names that have short vowel sounds, such as *cat, hen, pig, dog,* or *duck.* Write the corresponding vowels on each of the remaining lines. Little ones will sing this tune until the cows come home!

[Teacher's name] had a farm.
A-B-C-D-E.
And on [her] farm [she] had a [name of animal].
A-B-C-D-E.
With a [__, __] here,
And a [__, __] there,
Here a [__], there a [__], everywhere a [__, __].
[Teacher's name] had a farm.
A-B-C-D-E.

Mrs. Timmons had a farm.
A-B-C-D-E.
And on her farm she had a **pig**.
A-B-C-D-E.
With a p, p here,
And a p, p there,
Here a p, there a p,
   everywhere a p, p.
Mrs. Timmons had a farm.
A-B-C-D-E.

"Weight-ing" for Chicks

Balance out your farm unit with an activity that's sure to hatch a lot of knowledge. To prepare, transform eight yellow pom-poms into chicks by gluing a pair of wiggle eyes and an orange felt beak onto each one. Divide the chicks into pairs; then use hot glue to attach one penny to the bottom of each chick in the first pair. Stack and glue two pennies to each chick in the second pair, three pennies to each chick in the third pair, and four pennies to each chick in the last pair. Place each chick in its own plastic egg, place the eggs in an empty egg carton, and place the egg carton and a balance scale in a center.

At this center, a child weighs the eggs on the balance scale, trying to find the pairs with equal weights. To check for accuracy, she can open the eggs and count the pennies on each chick.

Sheep in All Sizes

Your youngsters will flock to create these adorable sheep. To prepare, draw and label three simple sheep (as shown) on a sheet of copy paper. Place cotton balls on each circle to determine the number needed to completely cover it. Then write the corresponding number inside each circle. Duplicate a class supply of the drawing on construction paper. Give each child a copy, a supply of cotton balls, and glue. Ask each youngster to cover each sheep body with the number of cotton balls indicated. Have her recheck her work before gluing the cotton balls in place and adding details to the picture with crayons.

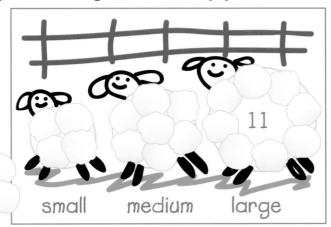

small   medium   large

Scrambled Eggs

Your little ones are sure to get "egg-cited" about this sequencing activity! Gather a dozen small plastic eggs. Use a permanent marker to label each egg with a different numeral from 1 to 12. Next, cut the bottom half of an egg carton into three-cup sections. Then divide the eggs into sets of three consecutive numerals. For example, the eggs labeled with 1, 2, and 3 will make one set, while another set will contain the eggs labeled 4, 5, and 6. Randomly place the eggs in each set into a separate egg carton section. To use, a child sequences each set of eggs in numerical order.

To further challenge youngsters, stamp a set of chicks onto a small construction paper egg to correspond to the numeral on each plastic egg. Have the child count the chicks on each paper egg and then insert it into the appropriate plastic egg. After you've checked for accuracy, scramble the eggs again for the next child.

The Farm

3 apples

2 broccoli

1 carrot

4 bananas

Barn-Raising Party

Raise some fun down on the farm with a barn-raising party. Tell your class that years ago barns were built by a team of farmers because it was a job too difficult for one to do alone. Then invite your little farmers to work in small teams to raise their own barns in the block center. Once each team has built its barn, invite the team to build fences for the plastic farm animals in the center. If desired, take an instant photo of each team enjoying its work and play around the barn. Then call in a demolition team to prepare the center for the next barn raising.

A Sing-Along Farmer Song

Your little ones will flock to the listening center to sing this special farmer's song—and be ready to come "baa-ck" for more later! In advance, make a tape recording of this song. Place the tape, along with the corresponding number of plastic animals named in the song, in your listening center. As youngsters visit the center, encourage them to round up the corresponding animals while quietly singing along to the tape.

(sung to the tune of "Old MacDonald Had a Farm")

[Teacher's name]'s class went to the farm,
E-I-E-I-O.
And at the farm we saw [one horse],
E-I-E-I-O.
With a [neigh-neigh] here, and a [neigh-neigh] there.
Here a [neigh], there a [neigh], everywhere a [neigh, neigh].
[Teacher's name]'s class went to the farm,
E-I-E-I-O.

Repeat the song, each time replacing the underlined number and animal with a different phrase: *two pigs, three sheep, four cows,* or *five chickens.* Also replace the animal sound with the sound corresponding to the named animal.

Farmer's Market

To market, to market, to buy a fat…fruit or vegetable! Transform your dramatic-play center into a farmer's market. Stock the center with baskets of plastic fruits and vegetables. (Or ask parents to send in real fruits and vegetables.) Then supply your marketplace with play money, a cash register, pencils and pads, grocery baskets, and paper bags. Next, prepare individual shopping lists for your children to use at the market. On each list, program a designated number of items, such as 3 apples, 6 potatoes, and 4 pears. To facilitate independence in reading the list, illustrate each item; then put the lists in your marketplace. Finally, invite students to open their farmer's market for business. Encourage them to take turns shopping for the groceries on their lists, running the cash register, writing receipts, and bagging the produce. The market's open—come shop 'til you drop!

Center Scarecrow

A simple scarecrow will be the perfect centerpiece for your literacy center. Invite small groups of children, in turn, to help make a scarecrow. To create the head, draw a face on one side of an inverted paper grocery bag; then stuff the bag with newspaper. Glue raffia onto the head for hair. To make the scarecrow body, put a flannel shirt on a metal clothes hanger; then stuff the shirt with newspaper. Fit a pair of overalls over the shirt, attaching the straps to the shirt with safety pins. Then stuff the overalls with newspaper, too. Tuck the bottoms of the pant legs into a pair of sneakers. Attach the head to the body by inserting the hanger's hook into the bag, then tying it tightly in place with a length of raffia or string. Top off the head with a straw hat; then place the scarecrow on a chair in your literacy center.

As each youngster visits the center, invite her to read a story to this friendly scarecrow. Or have each youngster draw a picture of something that frightens her. Then encourage her to present the drawing to the scarecrow so that he can scare away the frightening thing.

All Sorts of Farm Animals

Count on your little farmers to have all sorts of fun with this activity. Supply your sand table with a large assortment of plastic farm animals. (Provide six or more of each type of animal.) Use plastic fence pieces from a toy farm set to make several fenced areas in the sand. Or use plastic berry baskets with the bottoms cut off. Place a Styrofoam® meat tray with a die near the sand table. Then instruct each youngster to roll the die onto the meat tray. Have him count out a number of identical animals corresponding to the number on the die. Then ask him to place the animals in a fenced area. Encourage your little ones to continue rolling, sorting, and counting until all the little piggies—and their pals—are in their pens!

The Farm

Chores Round the Farm

Plant the seeds for better listening skills with this barnyard version of Telephone. First discuss the many types of chores a farmer does, such as milking the cow, driving the tractor, and seeding the fields. With your students sitting in a circle, whisper a chore in one child's ear. Then ask him to speak clearly as he whispers that same chore into the ear of the person to his right. Can the chore get passed around the circle successfully? Whether it does or not, invite everyone to act out the chore you named. Then continue to pass different chores until all the work gets done round the farm!

A Farmer's Life for Me

Get your students thinking about the life of a farmer with this ABC poem. As you recite the following poem, pass around a farm-related item, such as a packet of seeds, a plastic farm animal, or a toy tractor. At the end of the poem, have the child holding the farm item tell what he would like the most about living on a farm and what he would like the least. Recite the poem as many times as desired. Perhaps each of your youngsters will agree—"Farm living is the life for me!"

A-b-c-d-e-f-g,
A farmer's life is so busy.
H-i-j-k-l-and-m,
He goes from daybreak 'til day's end.
N-o-p-q-r-s-t,
Think how busy your life would be,
U-v-w-x-y-z,
If you lived on a farm with your family!

72

Designer Coats

Invite your little ones to design new coats for some favorite farm animals. Cut a large sheep, turkey, and cow from poster board. Display the cutouts on a wall or bulletin board within children's reach. Put a container of cotton balls under the sheep, a container of feathers under the turkey, and a container of quarter-sized paper circles under the cow. Select a student volunteer to stand in front of each animal. Give each volunteer a card with a numeral from 1 to 5 written on it; then have him count out the corresponding number of items from the container below his animal. Check each child for accuracy. Then brush glue onto a portion of each animal and have each child adhere his counted items. Repeat the activity until all your little designers have added to these new designer coats.

Countdown at the Henhouse
This countdown rhyme is "eggs-actly" what the teacher ordered!

[Five] little eggs all snug in a nest.
[Five] chicks inside are all at rest.

Peck, peck, peck—what's that I hear?
One little chick will soon appear!

Four little eggs…
Three little eggs…
Two little eggs…
One little egg…

Hold up [five] fingers.
Close hand and cover
*   with other fist.*

Pop one finger out of fist.

Funny Farm Sounds

You'll hear a "moo-moo" here and an "oink-oink" there with this animal-sounds game. In advance gather a picture of a farm animal for each child, and place each picture in an individual envelope. Distribute the envelopes, encouraging each child to keep his envelope's contents a secret. Next, give each child a turn to make the sound of his farm animal; then challenge classmates to identify the animal. Once everyone has had a turn, make a chorus of farm-animal sounds together.

How Now, Spotted Cow?

Show your little farmhands how to spot some cows with this beefy activity. To begin, have each youngster draw a large cow on a sheet of brown or white construction paper, or provide a simple cow pattern. Then give her a black bingo dabber and a length of thick brown or black yarn. Have the child repeatedly press the dabber on her cow to give it spots. Then have her attach a yarn tail to her cow. Show her how to unravel the free end of the yarn to make it resemble a cow's tail. Your little farmhands won't want to stop till the cows come home!

Play Dough Ponies

Invite your little ones to horse around with play dough to make their own breed of ponies. To prepare, gather play dough, a garlic press, a supply of craft sticks, and some green construction paper. Then show youngsters how to make a play dough pony. First have each child shape a pony's body and head from play dough balls. Then have him roll out a thick play dough snake between the palms of his hands. Instruct him to use a craft stick to cut the snake into four chunky legs. Help the child assemble his play dough pony (as shown); then invite him to squeeze some play dough through the garlic press to make the pony's mane and tail. Next, encourage your little farmhands to enclose their ponies in fences constructed from craft-stick rails and play dough posts. Finally, have youngsters provide their ponies with some torn construction paper grass for grazing.

"Hay!" It's a Scarecrow!

Your little farmers will have a "hay-day" when they create these silly scarecrows! Draw a circle, a square, and four small rectangles onto a sheet of copy paper; then make a construction paper copy of the sheet of shapes for each child. Give each child a copy of the shapes, a 12" x 18" sheet of construction paper, and a handful of hay. Have her cut out the shapes and glue them onto the construction paper to create a scarecrow as shown. Then direct her to glue some hay at the end of each of her scarecrow's arms and legs, and where its head and body meet. Invite her to use markers to add facial features to her scarecrow. Then encourage her to draw a field of cornstalks around her scarecrow to complete this fun farm scene.

Muddy Pigpens

Invite your children to roll up their sleeves and get elbow-deep in these muddy pigpens. In advance, duplicate a class supply of the pig pattern (page 195) on pink construction paper; then cut out and laminate each pig. Next prepare some instant chocolate pudding. Place the pudding, a spoon, the cutouts, large sheets of fingerpaint paper, and glue in your art center. Have each child at this center glue a cutout onto fingerpaint paper. Then invite her to spoon some pudding onto her paper. Encourage her to finger-paint a muddy pudding pigpen for her pig. When her pigpen is filled with plenty of cozy mud for her pig to wallow in, invite each child to lick her fingers clean!

Pickin' 'n' Peckin'

Do you hear a peck, peck here and a peck, peck there? Then your youngsters must have picked this fine-motor activity! To prepare, make a few copies of the chicken pattern (page 195) on tagboard; then color, cut out, and laminate each chicken. Position a red spring-type clothespin behind each cutout as shown; then hot-glue the clothespins in place. Place the completed chickens, a basket, paper plates, and a loaf of bread in a center. Invite each child in a small group to tear a slice of bread into several pieces onto a paper plate. Then encourage him to help a chicken peck its meal. Have the child open and close the chicken's clothespin beak to pick up the bread. Then have him deposit each piece of bread into the basket. When all the chickens have been fed, take the basket of bread outdoors to feed your other feathered friends.

The Farm

Farm Animal Antics

Head on over to the farm for some animal "moo-vements" sure to make your youngsters quack up! Encourage little ones to gallop like horses on all fours, then stop to shake flies off their tails! Or choose from the following list of farm animal antics. It's a hop hop here, and a kick kick there....

Waddle like a duck.
Roll in the mud like a pig.
Kick like a mule.
Strut like a turkey.
Hop like a bunny.
Stand like an ostrich.

Waddle.
Lie on floor; roll.
With hands on floor, kick feet in air.
Walk with hands tucked under armpits.
Hop on all fours.
Stand on one foot; tuck head.

Horsing Around

Have a hankering for some horseplay? Then make your own stick horses for frolicking around the farmstead. To make one stick, roll a sheet of newspaper diagonally; then tape it together. For the horse's head, cut two horse-head shapes from heavy tagboard. (Use a favorite pattern, if desired.) Place the two heads back-to-back. Then insert the newspaper stick between the two heads and staple them together. Invite youngsters to paint their sticks and color the faces on their horse heads. Then get ready to ride!

Hoedown

Yee-haw! It's time for a barn dance! Designate partners in advance. Then gather your country bumpkins in a circle with partners next to each other, and dance to the following song.

Swing Your Partner
(sung to the tune of "Old Brass Wagon")

Circle to the left, oh my darling,   *Hold hands; circle left.*
Circle to the left, oh my darling,
Circle to the left, oh my darling,
Time for the Hoedown Barn Dance.

Other verses:
Circle to the right, oh my darling…   *Hold hands; circle right.*
Move to the middle, oh my darling…   *Hold hands; walk to the middle and back.*

Swing your partner, oh my darling…   *Hook elbows and swing partner.*

Round 'em Up

Your little farmers will be singing 'til the cows come home with this musical movement activity. Have your youngsters walk in a circle as they sing the following song. Encourage the children to sing the tune again, substituting a cow's "Moo" for the words. Have them move around the circle like cows as they sing. Repeat the song, inserting a different animal and its sound in the last line, and leading children to move like that animal. After a few rounds, invite a student volunteer to complete the last line of the verse and lead the class in an animal movement.

Round the Farm
(sung to the tune of "Looby Loo")

Here we go round the farm.
Here we go round the farm.
Here we go round the farm.
Moo-ooing just like a cow.

[Moo, moo, moo, moo,
moo, moo…]

Farmer for a Day

Play this barnyard version of Simon Says to teach your little farmhands about chores down on the farm. Have youngsters follow your lead as you demonstrate the appropriate movements to accompany each chore. Don't eliminate any, or the chores won't get done!

Farmer says,
    "Milk the cow."
    "Feed the chickens."
    "Drive the tractor."
    "Gather eggs from the henhouse."
    "Plant the corn."
    "Pick apples."

The Farm

Top Slops

Ingredients:
1/3 cup applesauce per child
1 tablespoon raisins per child
1 tablespoon chopped dried apple per child
1 tablespoon grated carrot per child

Utensils and Supplies:
1 five-ounce paper cup per child
1 plastic spoon per child
1/3 cup measuring cup
1 tablespoon

Teacher Preparation:
Chop the necessary number of dried apple rings. Wash, peel, and grate the necessary number of carrots. Arrange the ingredients and utensils near the step-by-step direction cards.

There's no juice in a raisin!

What to Do When the Snack Is Through

What makes dried fruit different from fresh fruit? Help little ones find out with this science experiment. Set out some fresh grapes and some leftover raisins. Ask a small group of youngsters to examine the foods carefully. Explain that the raisins used to be grapes. Invite the children to offer explanations for how the grapes became raisins. Then use a sharp knife to cut into a few grapes and a few raisins. Ask youngsters to examine the fruit again. What do they see in the grapes that is missing from the raisins? What a juicy discovery!

Top Slops

wash
1

Applesauce
1/3 cup
measure and pour
2

RAISINS
TBSP
add 1
3

Dried Apple Slices
TBSP
add 1
4

TBSP
add 1
5

stir
6

The Farm

Moms and Babies on the Farm

Sing this song to help youngsters associate baby farm animals with their mothers. To prepare, gather toy farm animals corresponding to those in the song. (Or collect pictures for the animals in the song.) Distribute the parent-baby animal pairs to different volunteers. As you sing the song, encourage each child to hold up his animals at the appropriate time. Redistribute the animals to different children; then sing the song again so that each child has a turn to participate.

(sung to the tune of "He's Got the Whole World in His Hands")

We've got chickens and chicks
On our farm.
We've got horses and foals
On our farm.
We've got cows and calves
On our farm.
We've got moms and babies on our farm.

Sing additional verses about other farm families by substituting these animals in the song:

pigs and piglets
cats and kittens
dogs and puppies

goats and kids
sheep and lambs
turkeys and poults

Barnyard Buddies

Use a variety of farm animal pictures to set the "moo-ood" for this song. Each time you sing the verse, pause before saying an animal's name. Show students a picture of an animal; then invite them to insert that animal's name in the song.

(sung to the tune of "Clementine")

In the red barn, in the red barn,
In the red barn is a [horse].
In the red barn, on the big farm,
In the red barn is a [horse].

In the Barnyard

(adapted to the tune of "Skip to My Lou")

[Cow]'s in the barnyard.
[Moo! Moo! Moo!]
[Cow]'s in the barnyard.
[Moo! Moo! Moo!]
[Cow]'s in the barnyard.
[Moo! Moo! Moo!]
[Cow]'s at home in the barnyard.

To create new verses for this barnyard banter, simply substitute other farm animals and their sounds for the underlined words.

Fun on the Farm

(sung to the tune of "Pop! Goes the Weasel")

All around the big farmyard,
The farmer chased the [turkey].
The [turkey] thought it was all
in fun.
"[Gobble]," went the [turkey]!

Create additional verses by naming different farm animals and their corresponding sounds.

The Very Busy Farmer

(sung to the tune of "The Itsy-Bitsy Spider")

The very busy farmer
Works all the livelong day.
He milks the cows
And feeds the horses hay.
He gathers eggs and
Grows food that's the best.
Then the very busy farmer
Is ready for some rest!

The Farm

I Went Walking

You'll be surprised at whom you bump into as you stroll along with the young child in Sue Williams's *I Went Walking* (Harcourt Brace & Company). Have youngsters look for a clue in each illustration to help them predict which farm animal will appear on the following page. As a fun follow-up, cut a small square from a sheet of construction paper. Out of sight of the children, place a toy farm animal or a farm animal picture behind the opening in the paper so that only a portion of the animal shows. Encourage a student volunteer to say, "I went walking." Have the class respond, "What did you see?" Then have the volunteer guess the hidden farm animal and say, "I saw a [name of farm animal] looking at me." Remove the construction paper to reveal the hidden animal. Continue in this manner, reciting the text and guessing other hidden farm animals.

This Is the Farmer

Give your youngsters a taste of farm life by reading *This Is the Farmer* by Nancy Tafuri (Greenwillow Books). Set up a milking station to show your farmhands what it is like to milk a cow like the farmer does in the story. Place a bucket on top of newspaper or a towel. Fill a latex glove with water, and then wrap an elastic band around the opening of the glove. Use a straight pin to prick holes in the four fingertips (excluding the thumb). Next, use a permanent marker to draw a cat face on a plastic plate to represent the cat that gets a squirt of milk on the last page of the story. Tape the cat to the wall (next to the bucket) and cover the area below it with old towels or newspaper.

To use the milking station, one child holds the glove over the bucket, allowing the "teats" to dangle. Another child wraps four fingers around one "teat," with her thumb at the top. She firmly presses her thumb and index finger together to create pressure, and then slowly moves her fingers down until she squirts "milk" into the bucket. Once she has learned to "milk," have her try to aim a squirt of "milk" at the cat.

Going to Sleep on the Farm

A little boy asks, "How does a cow go to sleep?" and his father answers in *Going to Sleep on the Farm* by Wendy Cheyette Lewison (Puffin Books). This beautifully illustrated book has patterned and predictable text that your youngsters will soon catch on to. To help them enjoy the book further, make a classroom tape that will become a down-home favorite in your listening center. To prepare, read the book aloud several times, inviting the class to join in to provide the animal sounds and the "Shhh" sound at the end. After a few rehearsals, pop a blank tape into your tape recorder and read the book again with your students' help. Place the completed tape and a copy of the book in your listening center for all to enjoy.

Big Red Barn

Round up your little farmhands for a reading of *Big Red Barn* by Margaret Wise Brown (HarperCollins Publishers, Inc.). Call attention to the baby farm animals and their parents. Then follow up with your own simplified version of this barnyard tale. To prepare, program a sheet of copy paper with the text shown, leaving the blanks unprogrammed. Next, draw a simple barn shape (approximately 9" x 5") on another sheet of copy paper. For each child, photocopy the programmed page onto copy paper and the barn onto red construction paper. Cut out each barn and then make a T-shaped cut as shown. Glue the top and sides of each barn to a separate programmed sheet, above the text. Invite a child to fold open the barn doors and draw a mother farm animal and her baby inside the barn. Help him complete the sentence about his farm animals. Bind the completed pages into a class book titled "Our Big Red Barn."

In the big red barn there was a big _pig_ and a little _pig_.

Cock-a-doodle-doo: A Farmyard Counting Book

You'll reap a harvest of learning when you read *Cock-a-doodle-doo: A Farmyard Counting Book* by Steve Lavis (Lodestar Books). In advance, use the story text to create a read-along chart. Write "1 One noisy rooster" on the first line of a sheet of chart paper. Continue recording the lines of text in this manner until you have recorded all ten animals. Then cut a mouse head shape from brown craft foam to resemble the mouse in the story. Glue a wiggle eye on the mouse; then tape him onto the tip of a ruler to make a pointer. Reread the story, inviting a student volunteer to use the mouse pointer to point to the mouse on each page. Next, read the chart together as one student volunteer runs the mouse pointer under the words. Have another volunteer turn the corresponding pages of the book. On subsequent days, count on this chart to help you reinforce numerals, number words, or initial consonant sounds.

Garden

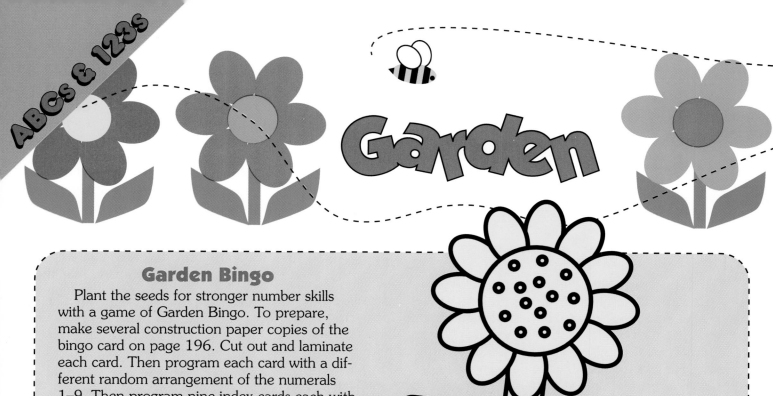

Garden Bingo

Plant the seeds for stronger number skills with a game of Garden Bingo. To prepare, make several construction paper copies of the bingo card on page 196. Cut out and laminate each card. Then program each card with a different random arrangement of the numerals 1–9. Then program nine index cards each with a numeral from 1 to 9 to serve as caller cards. To play, give each player a bingo card and nine sunflower seeds. Pick a caller card and call out the number. Each player covers that numeral with a seed. When a player covers three numerals in a row, he calls out "Seeds-O!" Youngsters will give this game two green thumbs up!

Seed Survival

Use this countdown rhyme to teach youngsters that only a small fraction of seeds actually get planted well enough to survive and thrive. As you recite the rhyme, ask students to hold up the corresponding number of fingers.

Five little seeds, blowing in the breeze,
Looking for a place to grow in peace.
One lands on ice. Too cold! He'll freeze.
Now four little seeds are blowing in the breeze.

Four little seeds, blowing in the breeze,
Looking for a place to grow in peace.
One lands on rock. No soil, you see.
Now three little seeds are blowing in the breeze.

Three little seeds, blowing in the breeze,
Looking for a place to grow in peace.
One lands in water. "Too wet!" says he.
Now two little seeds are blowing in the breeze.

Two little seeds, blowing in the breeze,
Looking for a place to grow in peace.
One lands in shade. But it's sun he needs.
Now one little seed is blowing in the breeze.

One little seed, blowing in the breeze,
Looking for a place to grow in peace.
He lands in soil that fits perfectly.
Now he'll grow into a healthy tree!

Garden Soup

Warm up youngsters' letter skills with today's special—garden-style alphabet soup. In advance, make die-cut letters from construction paper. Then distribute the letters to students. Help each child name a fruit or vegetable beginning with her letter. Have her illustrate that food on a notecard. Then label the back of her card with the food name. To make soup, recite the rhyme below, inviting each child to toss her letter and food card into a pot. Stir the soup to mix up the letters and cards. Then randomly pass a serving of soup—one letter and one food card—to each child. Together, sequence the letters; then have each child match her food card to the corresponding letter.

Pick and wash. Slice and toss.
Into the pot they go.
Add your special ingredients.
Now simmer it nice and slow!

Shapely Sprouts

Watch enthusiasm bloom as these flowers take shape right before youngsters' eyes. In advance, cut a quantity of construction paper shapes to represent different parts of a plant. You might cut small ovals for seeds, long rectangles for stems, hearts for leaves, circles for flower centers, and ovals for flower petals. Put the shapes in a center. Then send each child to the center to create a flower by gluing the shapes onto construction paper. During group time, invite the child to show his flower to the class. Ask him to name each shape represented in his flower. Then display the pictures on a bulletin board titled "Shapely Sprouts."

Grow a Rainbow

Invite your little sprouts to grow a garden of rainbow colors. In advance, make several tulip-shaped tagboard tracers. Invite each child to trace a tulip onto construction paper. Have her cut out the flower and glue it onto a craft stick stem. Then help her insert the flower into an inverted Styrofoam® cup to create a tulip planter. Collect all the planters; then invite each child, in turn, to sort and pattern the tulip colors as she desires.

85

Garden

Bees and Blooms

Invite youngsters to explore the "un-bee-lievable" relationship between the flower and the bee with this puppet rhyme. To begin, make a puppet stage by cutting out a window from the bottom of a large box (such as a copy-paper box); then paint the box green. After the paint dries, turn the box on its long side. Have students paint flowers on the box so that it resembles a flower garden. Next, duplicate the bee and flower patterns (page 197) on tagboard. Color and cut out each pattern; then glue wiggle eyes to each cutout. Tape each cutout to a craft-stick handle. Finally, tape-record this rhyme. Then place the stage, puppets, tape recorder, and tape in a center. Teach youngsters to use the puppets to perform the actions to the rhyme. Buzz!

Here's a pretty flower.	*Hold up flower.*
Here's a busy bee.	*Hold up bee.*
Each one needs the other,	
You soon will surely see.	
The flower needs the pollen	*Bee buzzes around the flower.*
The bee brings on her feet.	
The bee needs the nectar	
From flowers, oh so sweet.	*Bee lands on the flower.*
So when you see a buzzing bee,	*Hold up bee.*
Try not to make it "Shoo!"	*Make "shoo" motion.*
For it's honey from sweet nectar,	
She's making just for you!	*Point to audience.*

Seeds to Sow

Your little sprouts will enjoy watching as seeds grow into plants in your own mini garden. In advance, buy a variety of seeds, such as tomatoes, lettuce, radishes, and lima beans. Purchase a few aluminum foil muffin tins. Put the seeds and pans in your science center, along with potting soil, index cards (cut in half), craft sticks, and a spray bottle of water. Invite each child to plant a seed of his choice. Have him label a card with his name, then draw a picture of what his plant will look like when it's grown. Help him glue the card to a craft stick, then insert the stick into the muffin cup containing his seed. As a class, care for the mini garden until the seedlings are ready to be transplanted outdoors. Then cut the foil cups apart. Send each plant home with its owner to plant in his personal garden.

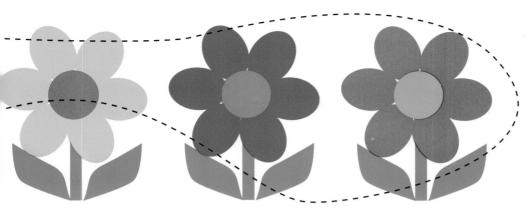

Play Dough Posies (and Roses and Tulips and Daisies...)

Creativity will stem from this play dough activity. In advance, gather several pastel colors of play dough. Provide flower-shaped cookie cutters and green pipe cleaners. Then invite children to cut out or create their own play dough flowers. Show them how to roll small balls of dough and flatten them to create flower centers and petals. Encourage them to complete their flowers with pipe cleaner stems and leaves.

Sand Table Garden

Have your little gardeners put their green thumbs to the test in your sand table. To prepare, collect children's plastic garden tools, garden gloves, straw hats, a watering can, a water-filled spray bottle, and several plastic flowers. Place the items near your sand table. As children visit the center, encourage them to dress in the hats and gloves for a day of gardening. Invite them to wet the "soil" with the spray bottle, then "plant" the flowers in the sand. Then have them pretend to water the flowers with the watering can. My, what a unique garden!

Glorious Garden

Your budding artists will plant themselves in the art center to make this floral mural. To prepare, cut a length of white bulletin board paper to use as the background. Gather a soft nylon shower "scrunchie," a foam dish mop, several lengths of corrugated bulletin board border, and bowls of paint. Roll up each bulletin board border tightly; then secure each roll with a rubber band. Cover an area of the floor with newspaper. Then place the paper and other materials on the newspaper. Encourage youngsters to dip the scrunchie, the dish mop, and the flat ends of the rolled border in paint, then press them onto the paper to create flowers. After the paint dries, have youngsters draw stems and leaves for their flowers. Display your mural in the hall; then watch the compliments bloom!

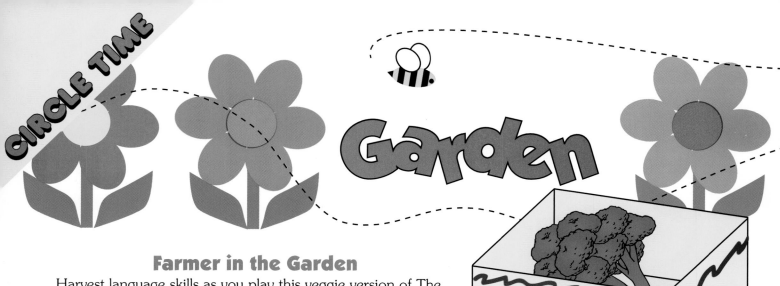

Garden

Farmer in the Garden

Harvest language skills as you play this veggie version of The Farmer in the Dell. In advance, make a vegetable necklace for each child. Duplicate a class supply of the vegetable patterns on page 198 onto colored construction paper; then cut them out. To make a necklace, punch a hole in the top of one vegetable cutout, thread a length of yarn through the hole, and knot the ends together. Distribute a necklace to each child and have him identify the vegetable on his necklace.

Have the students stand in a circle. Call one child to the center. Designate him as the farmer and give him a straw hat to wear. As you sing the following song, encourage the farmer to pick a child to join him in the circle and then insert the name of the vegetable that child is wearing into the song. Have all the children wearing that vegetable come to the center. Continue until all the vegetables have been picked. After singing the final verse, have students swap necklaces and send a new farmer veggie pickin'.

The farmer in the garden,
The farmer in the garden,
Heigh-ho, the veggie-o,
The farmer in the garden.

The farmer picks [potatoes].
The farmer picks [potatoes].
Heigh-ho, the veggie-o,
The farmer picks [potatoes].

Final verse
The farmer in the garden,
The farmer in the garden,
Heigh-ho, the veggie-o,
Harvesttime is here!

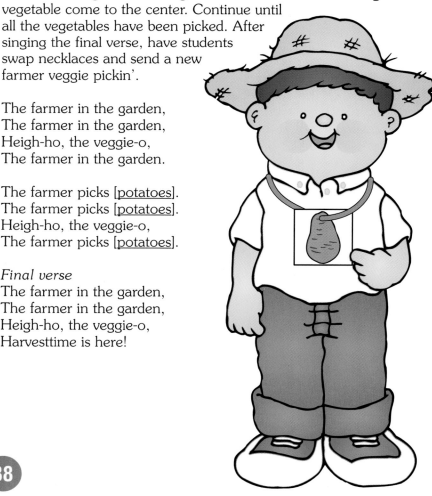

Mystery Veggie

It's no mystery—this activity will strengthen youngsters' critical-thinking skills! To prepare, duplicate and cut out the vegetable patterns on page 198. Each day during your garden unit, seal one fresh vegetable (one that is represented in the vegetable pictures) inside a shoebox. Display three of the vegetable pictures, including the one that represents the vegetable in the box. Pass the box around the circle. As you chant the following rhyme, have each child shake the box to get a sense of the vegetable's size, weight, and shape. Encourage students to comment about these characteristics. Once all the children have held the box, invite youngsters to guess which of the three vegetables is inside the box. Then reveal the mystery vegetable.

Something from the garden,
Which veggie can it be?
Listen to the sound it makes,
Before we look to see.

Today is ___Tuesday___

What is growing in my garden today?

In my garden, I have

Read All About It!

Grow a crop of readers with this daily prereading activity. To prepare, cut pictures of several different (familiar) vegetables and flowers from seed catalogs. (Or you might substitute copies of the vegetable patterns on page 198 for the pictures of vegetables.) Write the sentences below on a sheet of chart paper. Decorate the edges of the paper with drawings of flowers and vegetables if desired. Laminate the chart paper for repeated use. Next, write each day of the week on a separate tagboard strip, sized to fit on the first blank on your chart.

Each day during circle time, ask a student volunteer to tape the appropriate day-of-the-week strip to the chart. Then have her select a cutout and tape it to the chart as well. Encourage youngsters to identify the flower or vegetable selected. Then read the chart together, pointing to the words as you read.

> Today is _____.
> What is growing in my garden today?
> In my garden, I have _____.

Something Big From Something Small

Any way you slice it, this activity provides a fruitful science experience. Present a melon and a peach to your class. Discuss the size of each fruit. Ask youngsters to make some predictions about the seeds inside each fruit. Which fruit will have the larger seeds? Which will have smaller seeds? Then cut open the melon and scoop a spoonful of seeds onto a paper towel. Cut open the peach, remove the pit, and lay the pit next to the melon seeds. Talk about your students' predictions. Then brainstorm other examples of small fruits with large seeds, such as cherries, or large fruits with small seeds, such as grapefruit. Help students conclude that the size of the seed is not determined by the size of the fruit.

Bloomin' Bulb

Measurement skills will bloom as your little ones observe the growth of a bulb. Purchase a sprouted bulb from your local garden center. Gather a container of linking cubes and program a sheet of chart paper with the title "How Big Is Our Bulb?" At circle time, present the bulb to your class and explain that the children are going to measure the plant. Ask a student volunteer to connect enough linking cubes to equal the height of the plant; then count aloud the number of cubes used. Divide the class into pairs and have each pair connect the same number of cubes. Have each pair look for classroom items that equal the length of the cubes. Invite the children to bring the items to the circle. Attach those items that are lightweight to the chart paper. If children find items that are too heavy or immovable, write the names of those items on the chart. Repeat this activity periodically as your bulb continues to grow. Later, transplant the bulb outdoors to beautify your school or center grounds.

How Big Is Our Bulb?

Removable GLU-STIK

blue magnet

beanbag

block

Pretty Little Flowers All in a Row

Your little blossoms will have a ball making these fanciful flowers. In advance, supply your art center with 12" x 18" sheets of white construction paper, trays of paint in assorted colors, green markers, and a supply of scrap paper. Encourage each child to draw several flower stems of varying heights on his white paper; then have him add leaves to the stems. Challenge him to crumple a sheet of scrap paper into a ball using only one hand. Direct the child to dip the paper ball in a paint color; then have him press it onto his white paper to create a blossom on one of the stems he drew. Have him continue in this manner, crumpling a separate sheet of paper for each paint color, until each stem is topped with a flower. Before you know it, your art table will be in full bloom!

Greenhouse Gardens

Your little horticulturists will love digging in the dirt to create these indoor gardens. To prepare, obtain potting soil and three bean or radish seeds for each child. Gather a class supply of plastic liter soda bottles with lids. Set the lids aside until later. Cut off the bottom third of each bottle; then use a pushpin to poke several water drainage holes in each bottle bottom. Fill your sensory table with potting soil and some garden tools. Then give each child the top and bottom sections of a bottle. After some free exploration with the tools and soil, encourage each of your little sprouts to funnel soil through the inverted bottle top into the bottle bottom. Then ask her to poke three holes in the soil with her finger. Have her drop a seed into each hole, and then cover the seeds with soil. Instruct each child to water her seeds; then have her place the bottle top over the bottom. Screw the lid on to create a miniature greenhouse. Put the greenhouses in the window; then watch what sprouts from this potting project!

Garden

FINE MOTOR

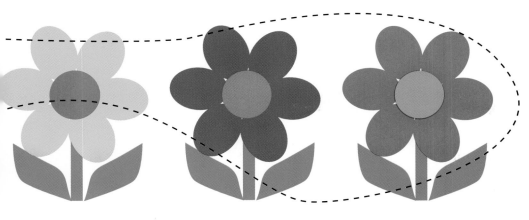

Clipping Flowers

Invite your little gardeners to strengthen their finger muscles when they clip these spring flowers. Gather sheets of tissue paper, several paper cups in spring designs or colors, and a large supply of clothespins in spring colors. (Or paint wooden spring-type clothespins in spring colors.) To begin, cut one-inch snips around the rim of each cup at one-inch intervals. Then bend each snipped section outward.

Place the cups, clothespins, and tissue paper in a center. To create a paper-cup flower, a child clips a clothespin to each bent section of a cup to form the flower's petals. Then he places a crumpled piece of tissue paper into the center of the cup to complete the flower. After he creates a garden full of blooms, have him return all the materials to the basket for the next gardener to use.

Garden "Wrap-ture"

Your budding gardeners are sure to get wrapped up in making these pretty posies. To prepare, collect a class supply of small paper plates in spring colors. Use a marker to draw a simple flower on each plate (as shown). Then cut a five-yard length of yarn for each child. Working with one small group at a time, have each child cut out the flower from a paper plate. Show her how to tape one end of a length of yarn to the back of her flower. Then invite her to wrap the yarn around her flower's center as she desires. When she reaches the end of her yarn, have her tape it to the back of the flower. For an added challenge, encourage her to cut a few lengths of curling ribbon, thread the ribbon under the wrapped yarn, and knot it. Show her how to use scissors to curl the ribbon. Wrap up this activity by mounting the finished flowers on a spring bulletin board.

Beans and Blooms

Fine-motor success and self-confidence are sure to stem from this garden project. In advance, take a close-up photo of each child (or photocopy his school photograph); then cut out the child's face. Provide each child in a small group with his photo, a sheet of 9" x 12" blue construction paper, construction paper in assorted colors (including yellow and green), scissors, glue, and a supply of dried beans. To make a flower, have each child trace a two-inch circle onto yellow construction paper and a six-inch flower shape onto another shade of paper. Have him cut out the shapes. (Provide precut shapes for younger children.) Have him glue his photo to the two-inch circle, and then glue the circle to the flower shape. Direct him to glue the flower shape near the top of his sheet of blue paper. Then have him add a green paper stem and leaves. Finally, invite the child to embellish his flower with beans glued on and around the different flower parts. Display your little flowering friends on a bulletin board titled "We're Blossoming!"

Garden

Plant Play

Your little sprouts will blossom as they follow your lead in this garden drama. For added effect, turn off the lights when you begin the drama; then turn them on as the seedlings break through the soil to bask in the sun.

You are a tiny seed tucked inside the soil.
Sit on the ground rolled up in a ball.
It is time to grow, so you send out tiny roots.
Slowly stretch feet out.
Your sprout begins to move up toward the sun.
Move arms up toward the ceiling.
You break through the soil!
Extend arms up and out.
The rain and sun make you feel strong.
Move to a squat position while reaching up.
You grow stronger and bigger every day.
Stand up with fully extended arms.
Until…you are a beautiful plant in the garden!

Garden Hose

Share the story *The Carrot Seed* by Ruth Krauss (HarperCollins Children's Books). Then invite your little gardeners to increase upper-body strength as they simulate pulling a giant carrot from the ground! Gather enough pairs of old hosiery for half the class. Cut the legs off the hosiery; then tie a knot at both ends of each leg. Have your youngsters spread out in an open space; then give each child a length of hosiery. Encourage each child to imagine he is holding a giant carrot as he tries these carrot-pulling actions:

- Stand on one end of hose with right foot. Pull the opposite end with the right hand. Repeat with left foot and hand.
- Stand on the center of hose with both feet. Hold a knot in each hand and pull up.
- Hold a knot in each hand with hose behind the back. Pull forward.
- Hold a knot in each hand with hose above the head. Bend at waist and pull side to side.

Now that you've planted the seed, let youngsters devise their own carrot-pulling actions!

Hit a Flower With Power

Help youngsters' aiming skills get on target with this tossing activity. To make a flower target, staple construction paper petals around the rim of a paper plate; then tape a red paper circle to its center. Mount the flower target on a wall at the eye level of a child. Tape a strip of masking tape to the floor four feet in front of the target. Place a basket of beanbags near the tape. Have a child step up to the line and toss each beanbag at the flower, attempting to hit the red center. That's flower power!

Wiggle-Worm Workout

Don't step on this wiggle worm! His wiggling and youngsters' jumping will loosen the garden soil! Stretch a jump rope across the ground and ask your youngsters to imagine it is a worm. With the help of another adult, hold the rope close to the ground while rapidly wiggling it from side to side. Have groups of two or three children jump back and forth over the rope, trying not to squoosh the worm.

Pick Me!

Your little blossoms will pop up to be picked when singing this flowery version of "London Bridge." In advance, have each child make a corsage by cutting a simple flower shape from construction paper. Use masking tape to fasten each child's flower to his clothing. To play the game, join hands with an adult assistant to make a bridge. Have the children form a line to go under and around the bridge as you sing the following song:

(sung to the tune of "London Bridge")
Picking flowers in the spring,
Orange, yellow, red, and green.
Picking flowers pink and blue,
Now I'll pick you!

As you sing, "Now I'll pick you!," drop the bridge and capture the child underneath in your arms. Strengthen color recognition by asking the class to identify the color of the flower worn by the child. Continue playing until there isn't a single flower left to be picked!

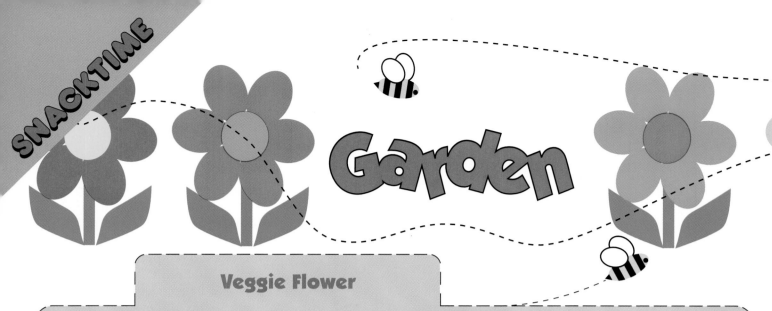

Garden

Veggie Flower

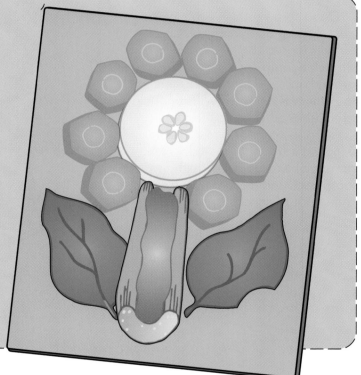

Ingredients:
1 cucumber slice per child
8 carrot rounds per child
1/2 celery stalk per child
peanut butter
2 salad leaves (such as spinach) per child

Utensils and Supplies:
1 plastic knife (or craft stick) per child
napkins
vegetable peeler
knife

Teacher Preparation:
Wash the celery stalks; then trim the ends and cut them in half. Peel and slice the necessary number of cucumbers and carrots. Wash the salad leaves. Arrange the ingredients and utensils near the step-by-step direction cards.

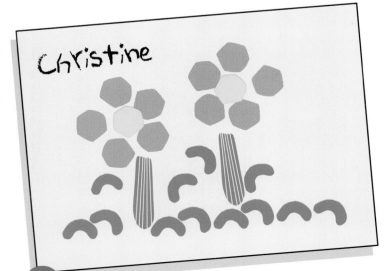

Christine

What to Do When the Snack Is Through

Watch smiles blossom as your little sprouts use left-over celery and carrots to create garden paintings. Set out construction paper and a few colors of tempera paint. Invite each child to use the length of a celery stalk to print stems, and the end of a cut carrot to print flower centers and petals. Have her add leaves and grass by printing with the end of a celery stalk. Pretty!

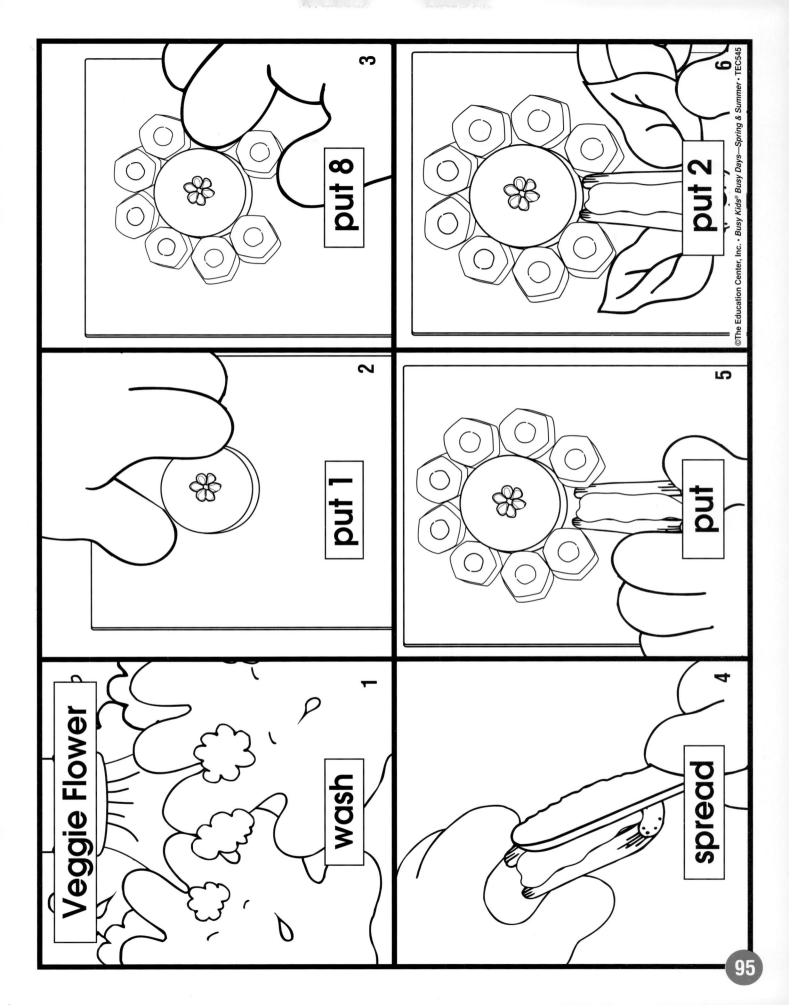

Veggie Flower

wash — 1

put 1 — 2

put 8 — 3

spread — 4

put — 5

put 2 — 6

Garden

The Itsy Bitsy Seedling

Sprout some fingerplay fun with these simple seedling puppets. To make one, cut a simple seedling from green construction paper. Glue the cutout onto a craft stick. Then invite each child to use his puppet as he recites this fingerplay.

(sung to the tune of "The Itsy Bitsy Spider")

The itsy-bitsy seedling
Grew up through the ground.

Make a loose fist with left hand.
Push seedling up through fist; tighten hand to secure.

Down came the rain
To wet it all around.

Wiggle fingers on right hand.
Circle fingers around seedling.

Out came the sun
And warmed it through and through.

Spread out fingers on right hand.
Wave right hand over seedling.

And the itsy bitsy seedling
Grew an inch or two.

Push seedling up further through fist.

One row of carrots,

Two rows of peas,

Three rows of lettuce,

In my garden, you see.

Four rows of cucumbers,

Five of tomatoes.

And over to the side,

Six rows of potatoes.

When it's time to harvest,

A feast there will be,

As I share my garden goodies

With my happy family!

Fresh From the Garden

Plant a little knowledge about garden foods in your youngsters' minds with this counting poem. In advance, cut from garden catalogs or magazines a picture of each food mentioned in the poem. Then copy the poem onto chart paper. Glue each food picture next to its name. As you read the poem, invite your class to "read" along, naming each garden food.

Pick a Bunch of Flowers

(sung to the tune of "Pick a Bale of Cotton")

Gonna jump down, turn around,
Pick a bunch of flowers;
Jump down, turn around,
Pick a bunch today.

Oh, garden!
Pick a bunch of flowers.
Oh, garden!
Pick a bunch today!

If desired, create new verses by replacing *flowers* with names of flowers, such as *daisies, roses,* and *tulips.*

Daisy Math

Reinforce subtraction skills with this darling daisy rhyme. Have youngsters use their fingers to count down the petals remaining on the daisy. Be sure to pause during the third line to allow your little ones time to supply the answer.

Five petals on my daisy.	*Hold up five fingers.*
If I pluck one away—	*Fold down one finger.*
That leaves **four** petals	*Show four fingers.*

On my daisy today.

(Repeat the verse, substituting the appropriate number words and actions each time. Then recite the last verse to conclude the rhyme.)

No petals on my daisy.
I've plucked them all away.
Only one thing I can do—
Pick another one today!

Garden

Sunflower House

One child's active imagination turns an ordinary sunflower garden into a sunflower house and more in Eve Bunting's *Sunflower House* (Voyager Picture Books). For a flowery follow-up, invite your little seedlings to grow into beautiful sunflowers with the help of this action rhyme. Seat the children in a circle; then set a plastic sandwich bag with a few sunflower seeds in front of each child. Encourage youngsters to follow along as you lead them in the suggested motions.

Pull up the weeds.	*Make pulling motion with hands.*
Sow all the seeds.	*Take one seed from bag and pretend to plant.*
Water them every day.	*Pretend to hold a garden hose.*
Stems grow fast.	*Crouch; then stand tall.*
Flowers here at last!	*Put hands together overhead.*
A sunflower house! Hooray!	*Lean toward center of circle with hands overhead.*
At summer's end,	
Flowers start to bend,	*Bend at waist; pour seeds out of bag onto floor.*
So, I store their seeds away!	*Sit and collect seeds in bag.*

Dandelion Adventures

What happens when the wind sends tiny dandelion seeds flying into the air? Read aloud *Dandelion Adventures* by L. Patricia Kite (The Millbrook Press, Inc.) to find out. After reading the story, invite youngsters to make their own dandelions from clay. To prepare, cut enough cotton swabs in half so that each child will have seven. Give each child his seven cotton-swab halves, a small ball of clay, and a craft stick. To make a dandelion, the child pushes his craft-stick stem into the clay. Then he gently inserts the cut ends of the swabs around the perimeter of the clay ball. As you re-read the story, invite youngsters to use their dandelions to practice simple subtraction. As each seed parachute flies and lands somewhere, have each youngster make one swab fly away and land in front of him. Then have the child count to see how many seed parachutes are left on the dandelion. Be sure to help youngsters compare their subtraction with the dandelion picture provided at the bottom of each page. Have youngsters continue in this manner until all seven seed parachutes have landed. If desired, collect all the dandelion seed parachutes and have older children count them to see how many dandelion seeds were dispersed altogether. Now *that's* some dandy math practice!

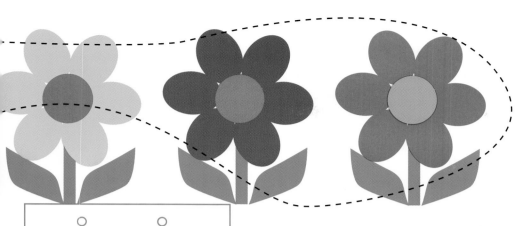

Flower Garden

After sharing *Flower Garden* by Eve Bunting (Harcourt Brace & Company), talk about the beautiful garden box that the young girl made for her mom's birthday. Then treat your youngsters to this deliciously edible flower garden. In advance, prepare a batch of chocolate pudding. Gather and prepare two or three of the following fruits (or other colorful seasonal fruits): whole fresh strawberries, whole grapes, kiwi slices, or orange slices. Give each child a sturdy paper cup, a plastic spoon, an Oreo® cookie, and a green craft stick. Have each child spoon some pudding into his cup. Then have him crumble his cookie over his pudding and mix it together with his spoon. Next, have him insert his craft-stick stem into a desired piece of fruit and then plant the flower in his pudding mix soil. Place the fruity fowers side by side in a large shoebox to resemble the beautiful garden box from the story. Take a picture; then invite the children to enjoy their incredible, edible flowers.

Amy – Apple
David – Dandelion
Emma – Eggplant
Faiza – Forget-me-nots
Henry – Hollyhock
Penny – Pumpkin
Reneè – Rose
Sam – Sunflower
Tracy – Tulip
Zachary – Zinnia

Alison's Zinnia

"Alison acquired an Amaryllis for Beryl. Beryl bought a Begonia for Crystal." And so the story grows in a flowery alphabet book called *Alison's Zinnia* by Anita Lobel (Mulberry Books). As you share the book, note the language pattern on each page. Then invite your children to make a class book linking their own names with things that grow in a garden. Begin by listing the children's names in alphabetical order on a sheet of chart paper. Ask each child to think of a garden flower, fruit, or vegetable that begins with the same letter as his name; then record his response next to his name. Next, insert the child's name and his selected garden item into a sentence similar to those in the book on the bottom of a sheet of white construction paper. Be sure to complete the sentence with the next child's name from your alphabetical list. Prepare a sheet for each child in this same manner. (For the last child on your list, complete the sentence by inserting the first child's name on the list.) Ask youngsters to illustrate their sentences; then bind the pages together into a clever class book.

Jack's Garden

Jack's Garden by Henry Cole (Mulberry Books) will inspire your little gardeners to grow their very own class garden. First, decide on the garden location, such as in the schoolyard or in a water table (or plastic window box) filled with potting soil. Follow Jack's gardening steps from the book. Prepare the soil, plant the seeds, and then add some rain with a spray bottle. While waiting for the plants to grow, invite your little ones to complete a cumulative garden booklet similar to the story. Photocopy a class supply of the reproducible on page 194. Make a booklet for each child by stapling five half sheets of copy paper together. Have each child cut apart the sentences on his copy of the reproducible. Have him look at the numerals in front of each sentence and then glue one sentence strip to each page of his booklet, in numerical order. Read aloud the first four pages and encourage youngsters to add illustrations. Set the booklets aside. When the garden has finally grown, revisit the booklets and have students complete them by drawing the class plants on the last page. See the pride that blossoms from the plants that grew after the rain that wet the seeds....

4. This is the rain that watered the seeds that we planted in the soil that made up the garden our class planted.

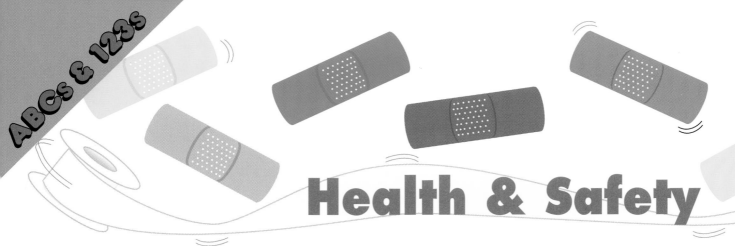

Health & Safety

Play It Safe

Use this street-smart safety rhyme to reinforce the concept of left and right. To help children distinguish between their left and right sides, teach them this simple trick. Have each child hold the back of his left hand in front of him as shown. Point out that his left hand makes an *L*, the letter at the beginning of the word *left*. Then say the rhyme. Have youngsters perform the actions. As needed, encourage them to use the special trick as a reminder of their left sides. Now that's the right way to teach about left and right!

Left, right, left.
I'm walking with my feet.
Left, right, left.
I'm stopping at the street.
Left, right, left.
I'll look before I go.
Left, right, left.
Just look at what I know.

Walk left, right, left.

Walk left, right, left; then stop.

Turn head left, right, left.

Walk left, right, left.

Chicken Pox Spots

Are youngsters curious about the common childhood disease known as chicken pox? If so, scratch the surface of this topic with these spot-counting pictures. To begin, invite each child who has had this itchy illness to share his experience with the class. Ask him to tell about some things that made him feel better when he was sick, such as taking an oatmeal bath, wearing mittens to prevent him from scratching his scabs, or getting a hug from Mom. Conclude your discussion by telling youngsters that chicken pox is caused by a virus—not chickens! One requires special care and time to recover from this illness. Then have each child draw a self-portrait. Write a numeral on each picture; then laminate it. Put the pictures and a red wipe-off marker in a center. Invite each center visitor to select a classmate's portrait. Then have him draw the number of chicken pox spots on the portrait to correspond to the numeral on the page. Youngsters are sure to giggle their way through this silly game about an illness with a silly name.

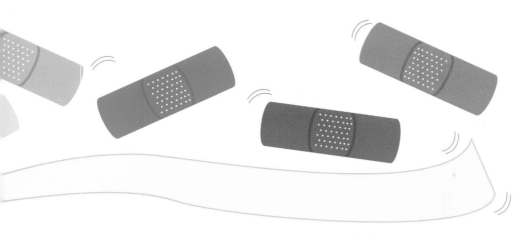

"Alpha-cises"

Staying fit is as easy as ABC when your exercise regime includes this alphabetical workout. To warm up, ask a volunteer to lead the class in a simple exercise, such as toe touches, side bends, or running in place. Encourage youngsters to keep doing the named exercise until they've rhythmically recited the entire alphabet. Then ask another volunteer to lead the group in a new exercise and a second recitation of the ABCs.

For some "alpha-cises" with a creative twist, divide the class into groups of three or four students. Call out a letter of the alphabet; then encourage youngsters to form that letter with their bodies, either individually or as a group. After a round of "alpha-cises," youngsters will feel more healthy in mind and body!

Happy Hand Washing

Teach your little ones to be germ busters with this sequencing activity. In advance photograph a different child performing each of several hand-washing steps. For example, you might picture one child turning on the water, another lathering her hands, a third child rinsing her hands, a fourth child turning off the water, a fifth child drying her hands, and a sixth child throwing a paper towel in the trash can. Laminate the photos for durability. During group time, discuss each photograph in sequence; then place the pictures in a center. Encourage students to sequence the photos as they explain the steps to proper hand washing. Later, display the sequenced pictures near your classroom sink to remind youngsters of the how-tos of hand washing.

Pass the Tissue, Please

Share this poem to reinforce the importance of using tissues to prevent the spread of germs. To prepare, write the poem on chart paper; then recite it several times with your class. Once youngsters are familiar with the poem, write each line on a separate sentence strip. Give each of five children a strip. Encourage them to sequence the strips as they recite the poem. Repeat this procedure until each child has had a turn. Then, to increase the challenge, cut apart the words on each sentence strip. Have youngsters take turns sequencing the words in each line of the poem. Be sure to display the chart as a reference.

Ahh-ahh! There's a tickle in my nose.
Ahh-ahh! Now what do you suppose?
Ahh-ahh! I think I'm going to sneeze.
Ahh-ahh! I need a tissue, please.
Ahh-ahh…Ahh-choo!

Ahh-ahh! There's a tickle in my nose.

Ahh-ahh! Now what do you suppose?

Ahh-ahh! I think I'm going to sneeze.

Ahh-ahh! I need a tissue, please.

Ahh-ahh... Ahh-choo!

101

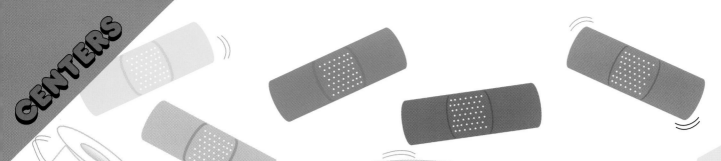

Health & Safety

STOP

Signs of Safety

Give your little ones a reason to STOP and notice traffic signs by making your own for the block center. To begin, draw an assortment of road signs—such as *Stop, Yield, Speed Limit,* and *Railroad Crossing*—on appropriate tagboard shapes. (Or, for an even more realistic look, cut the signs from a driver's handbook; then mount the cutouts on tagboard.) Glue each sign to one end of a craft stick. Use plaster of paris to anchor the other end of each craft stick inside a plastic top from a laundry detergent bottle. After the plaster dries, place the signs in your block center. They're sure to be real traffic stoppers!

Wash Those Hands!

Set up your discovery center to help youngsters discover the importance of washing their hands. Provide brown tempera paint, several brushes, a supply of paper towels, and a supply of white copy paper. Invite a child who visits the center to first label a sheet of paper with his name. Then have him paint the palm of one hand with the brown paint. Have him wipe his hand off with a paper towel, then make a handprint on one side of his paper. Then have him go to the sink, wash his hands with soap and water, and dry them. Have him return to the center and make another handprint next to the first one. If the paint were dirt, which method was more effective in removing it—wiping his hands or washing them? If desired, print the message "Wash Those Hands!" on each child's paper and send it home to spark a discussion.

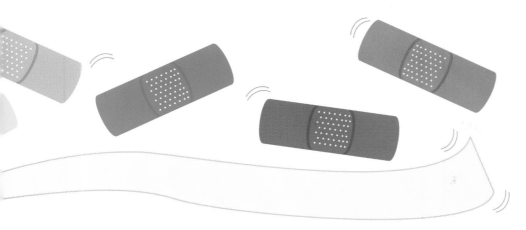

What's Up, Doc?

Doctor up your drama center by setting up a medical clinic. To begin, gather several toy doctor kits. Or ask the school nurse or parents in the medical profession to donate items such as lab coats (or oversized, white dress shirts), plastic syringes, empty pill bottles, stethoscopes, gauze, bandages, and ice packs. Place the supplies in your dramatic-play center. Set up a few chairs to serve as the waiting room area and a cot or nap mat to use as the examination table for patients. Ready? The doctor is in!

Red Light, Green Light

Students will *stop* what they're doing to *go* to this safety-awareness center! In advance, make a tagboard copy of the safety cards on page 199; then color and cut apart the cards. If desired, laminate them for durability. Open a manila file folder and draw a red circle on one side of the fold and a green circle on the other side to represent traffic lights. Store the picture cards inside the folder. Invite each youngster who visits this center to open the folder and sort the cards. Have him place the cards that show safe actions on the green traffic light and the cards that show unsafe actions on the red traffic light. After this activity, youngsters will be "en-light-ened" about safety!

Erasing Cavities

Help little ones brush up on dental hygiene with this center activity that's guaranteed to make them smile. To begin, affix pieces of white plastic tape to your chalkboard to create a big, toothy grin. Cut out a tagboard toothbrush about the size of a chalkboard eraser; then tape the cutout to the back of a chalkboard eraser. Invite visitors to the center to use colored chalk to draw particles of food on and between the white-tape teeth. Then have them use the toothbrush-eraser to brush off the traces of cavity-forming foods. Let's see those pearly whites now!

Health & Safety

Sneaky Snack

Give your students practice selecting foods that promote good dental health. Show the children a variety of fruits and vegetables that are good for teeth—such as a carrot, an apple, or a celery stick. Then display samples of foods that are not so good for teeth—such as a candy bar, jelly beans, or a cookie. Collect all of the food items in a basket. Tell your students you need their help in identifying the sugary snacks that are sneaking their way into your collection of healthful snacks. Display three snacks at a time: two that represent good dental-health choices and one that represents a poor choice. Ask the children to identify the sneaky, sugary snack. Continue until you've eliminated all the sweets from your treats.

Counting With the Tooth Fairy

Practice counting and listening skills with the help of some tooth-fairy magic. Put aside a small bell. Place one plastic cup and five Styrofoam® peanuts—to represent teeth—in front of each child. Invite the children to pretend they are tooth fairies. Explain that the tooth fairies are going on a tooth-collecting trip. Have the children count the number of times they hear you ring the bell and place the corresponding number of teeth in their cups. Check for accuracy by asking each child to count the number of teeth he has in his cup. With each house the tooth fairies visit, have them empty their cups and listen for a different number of teeth to collect.

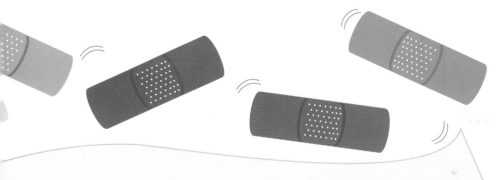

Get Up and Go

Wake your kids up to some fire-safety rules. Purchase an inexpensive battery-operated smoke alarm. (Or make a paper model from a white paper plate with a red construction paper button.) With a puppet on one hand, ask the students to observe the puppet to see if it knows what to do in a fire. Push the test button to sound the alarm; then make the puppet hide beneath your arm. Encourage the children to convince the puppet that hiding is the wrong thing to do. Stress this rule: in case of a fire, get out and stay out! To reinforce this lesson, teach the children the following song. Then have them pretend to be sleeping while you sound the alarm again. Line up to practice leaving the building.

Fire-Safety Song
(sung to the tune of "Are You Sleeping?")

While you're sleeping,
While you're sleeping,
Beep! Beep! Beep!
Beep! Beep! Beep!
The smoke alarm is ringing.
The smoke alarm is ringing.
Out of bed!
Move your feet!

Brush Your Teeth

Teach your youngsters to take the time that is necessary to have a fresh, bright smile. Set a small sand timer or kitchen timer before the children. Explain that to do a complete job of brushing, it is best to brush for three minutes. Then use a pretzel stick as a toothbrush to demonstrate how to brush your teeth properly. Give each child his own pretzel stick, set the timer, and lead the children in a three-minute brushing session. Then invite your little dental students to eat their makeshift toothbrushes!

Hello, 911?

Practice dialing 911 in this role-playing activity that's a lifesaver. Write "911" in large numerals on your chalkboard. Bring two toy telephones to circle time: one for yourself and one for a child. Discuss the importance of calling 911 in an emergency. Create an emergency scenario and explain it to the class. Select one child to dial "911" and report the emergency to you—the dispatcher—as you listen on the other phone. Encourage the child to speak clearly and to give her full name and address. Then give her a certificate that says "I'm number one at calling 911." Provide other youngsters with the opportunity to practice emergency calls during fire-safety week.

Health & Safety

"Sew" Safe

This lacing activity is a safe bet for fine-motor practice. To make a stop-sign lacing card, cut a large octagon from red poster board. Use a black marker to write "STOP" in the center of the cutout. Then laminate the sign for durability. Place the sign on a Styrofoam® block; then use a nail to poke evenly spaced holes along the lines of each letter. Cut a length of white yarn long enough to lace in and out of all the holes. Dip one end of the yarn into glue and let it dry. Then thread the opposite end into the first hole in the letter S and tie a knot to secure it. Invite a child to sew the yarn through the letters on the sign. When he's finished, invite him to pull out the yarn to ready the activity for the next child. Once your youngsters get going on this activity, they'll find it hard to STOP!

The Picture of Health

Can your youngsters spot a healthy habit? Find out with the reproducible on page 200. Give each child a copy of page 200; then encourage your students to color all the pictures. Discuss with the class the healthy and unhealthy habits shown in the pictures. Have each child use a yellow crayon to circle the pictures of healthy habits. Then have him use a black crayon to mark an X through each picture of an unhealthy habit. Ask him to cut out all the pictures. Then have him sort the cutouts into two groups: healthy habits and unhealthy habits. Invite him to glue the healthy habits onto a sheet of paper with the caption "Remember to…" Then ask him to rip up the unhealthy pictures and toss those bad habits away!

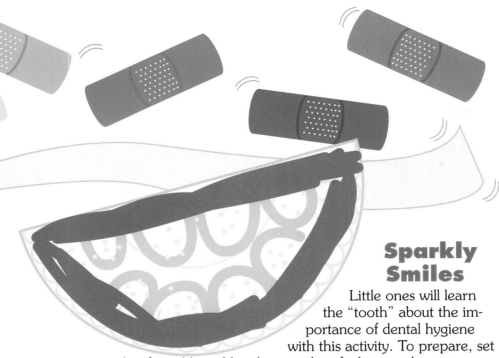

Sparkly Smiles

Little ones will learn the "tooth" about the importance of dental hygiene with this activity. To prepare, set up a center with a few old toothbrushes, a tube of white toothpaste, crayons, and iridescent glitter in a shaker bottle. Cut one large paper plate in half for every two students. Give each child at this center a plate half; then ask her to imagine that it is a smile. Have her color a set of lips around the edge of her plate. Then have her draw two rows of teeth in the mouth. Next, direct her to squeeze some toothpaste onto a toothbrush and then brush the toothpaste onto her paper-plate teeth. While the toothpaste is still wet, invite her to sprinkle a bit of iridescent glitter on the teeth. Finally, invite youngsters to take their projects home to show their families how brushing creates a sparkly smile!

Germ Free

Answer your youngsters' questions about the gloves worn by health care professionals with this hands-on exploration. To begin, gather a supply of disposable plastic gloves. Show a pair of gloves to the class; then discuss who wears them and why. Afterward, invite children to visit your art center to discover how the gloves keep hands clean. Place several trays of fingerpaint, fingerpaint paper, and the disposable gloves in your art center. Ask each child at the center to slip a glove onto one hand; then have him place both hands into a tray of paint. Invite him to create a fingerpaint masterpiece on a sheet of paper. Then have him remove the glove and compare his two hands. Why do health care workers wear gloves? The answer will be as plain as the paint on your hand!

A Hot Spot for Safety

Spot-check your little ones' fire-safety knowledge with this cut-and-paste activity. In advance, enlarge and duplicate a class supply of the dalmatian dog pattern on page 201 onto white construction paper. Discuss fire-safety rules with your class, highlighting all the procedures they need to follow in case of a fire. Then invite small groups to join you for a fire-safety review and craft session, too!

Have each child cut out a dalmatian pattern. Then give him four or five black construction paper circles to hold. Spot-check his knowledge of fire safety by asking him to share something he learned from the class discussion. Each time he recalls a fire-safety rule, invite him to glue a black spot onto his dalmatian. Once all the dogs are spotted, send them home and ask the children to share this hot topic with their families.

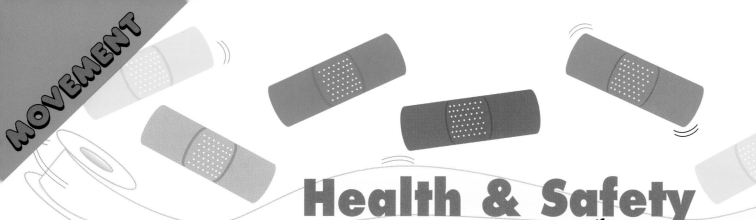

Health & Safety

Stop for Safety

At the beginning of the year, a most appropriate gross-motor activity is getting youngsters familiar with your playground equipment. Help your little ones use the equipment safely with this tip. Cut one red and one green octagon from poster board. Label the red octagon "Stop" and the green one "Go." Tape a paint-stirring stick to the back of one shape; then staple the signs back-to-back.

As you explain how to use each piece of playground equipment, invite a few volunteers to demonstrate its use. Flash the "Go" sign if they use the equipment safely, and offer lots of praise. Flash the "Stop" sign if you see a problem, such as a child standing in front of the swings while they're in use. Remind all the students of the proper use of that piece of equipment. After students are familiar with your Stop-and-Go sign, you can use it during playground time for the first weeks of school and periodically throughout the year as a review.

A Toothy Grin

Need to brush up on dental-hygiene skills? How about a mouth full of giant teeth to practice on? To make giant teeth, have the children paint the outside of large paper grocery bags with white tempera paint. When the paint is dry, slip each paper-bag tooth over the back of a chair. Put the chairs in a row; then give each child a clean, old toothbrush to "brush" the teeth. Play Raffi's "Brush Your Teeth" and encourage youngsters to brush to the beat. As an extension, give pairs of children strands of white yarn and have them "floss" between the teeth. It's sure to make your little ones smile!

Old-Time Bucket Brigade

Celebrate fire-safety week with this relay game commemorating the old-time bucket brigade. On a warm day, take your youngsters outdoors and divide them into several groups. Designate a starting line and a finish line that are ten feet apart. For each group, place a bucket of water at the starting line and an empty bucket at the finish line. Have each group line up behind a bucket at the starting line. Give each child a small plastic cup. Explain that each child should fill his cup with water from the first bucket, carry the cup to the second bucket without spilling it, then empty the water into the second bucket and run back to the end of her line. Yell, "Fire! Fire! Fire!" to start the game. Cheer your fire-fighters on as they cross the finish line!

Wake-Up Call

Reinforce healthy hygiene habits with some morning mime. First, help the children devise panto-mime motions for morning routines, such as combing hair and brushing teeth. Then invite two or three children at a time to come forward for their wake-up call. Call out three consecutive commands such as, "Get dressed. Eat a healthy breakfast. Brush your teeth." Then watch to see if the children follow the commands, pantomiming them in the proper sequence.

Stop, Drop, and Roll

Stop! Drop everything and practice this red-hot safety routine. To begin, invite youngsters outside to run in an open grassy area. Then head indoors for a discussion. Ask youngsters what they felt on their faces and arms as they ran. Guide them to understand that they felt the air rushing by as they ran. Then relate their experience to fire safety. Explain that fire needs air—just like the air they felt on their faces and arms—in order to burn. Ask what they think they should do if their clothes catch fire. Should they run? Point out that running—or even walking—will provide lots of air for the fire and help it burn. Then explain the stop, drop, and roll technique for extinguishing a clothing fire. Tell children that rolling on the ground will cut off the air supply and help put out the fire.

Demonstrate the technique on a mat or a carpeted area. Then give each child a chance to practice this lifesaving technique. Practice and repetition will make your class fire-smart!

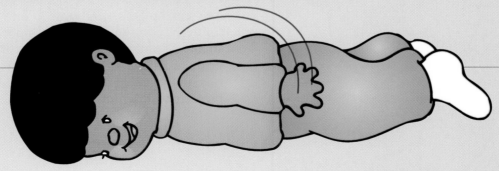

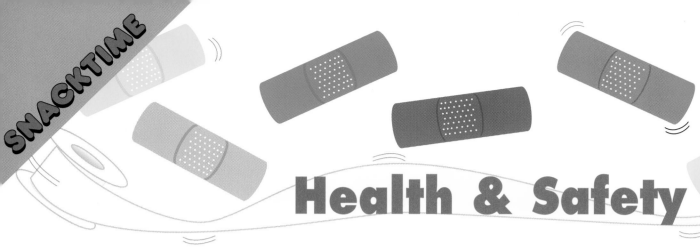

Health & Safety

Stop 'n' Drop Roll

Ingredients:
1 slice of bread per child
peanut butter
jelly

Utensils and Supplies:
1 plastic knife (or craft stick) per child
napkins
2 spoons
knife

Teacher Preparation:
   Trim the crusts from each slice of bread. Arrange the ingredients and utensils near the step-by-step direction cards.

What to Do When the Snack Is Through

   Stop! Don't throw away those bread crusts. Use them—and any leftover bread slices—to make some easy sculpting dough. Crumble up the crusts and slices into small pieces. Then mix in one teaspoon of glue for every one-fourth cup of crumbs. Give each child a small ball of the mixture to shape into a tiny pinch pot or other shape. Leave the sculptures to dry and harden overnight. If desired, decorate the dried projects with tempera paint.

Health & Safety

Scrub-a-Dub

Before snack or lunchtime, hand over healthy habits to your little ones with this squeaky-clean hand-washing song. If desired, have youngsters continue washing their hands as they repeat the verse, substituting a repetitive "la-la" for the words. This will ensure that youngsters scrub their hands long enough to get them *really* clean!

(sung to the tune of "Clap, Clap, Clap Your Hands")

[Child's name], [child's name], wash your hands,
Wash them 'til they're so clean.
Scrub, scrub, scrub-a-dub,
The cleanest hands you've seen.

Buckle Up!

Steer youngsters in the right direction with this song about car safety. After learning the words, encourage your little safety supervisors to sing it to their families as they prepare for car rides. If desired, send a copy to parents to encourage them to reinforce this important lesson with their children.

*(sung to the tune of
"Happy Birthday to You")*

Buckle up for safety.
Buckle up for safety.
Wear your seat belt, dear [child's name].
Buckle up for safety.

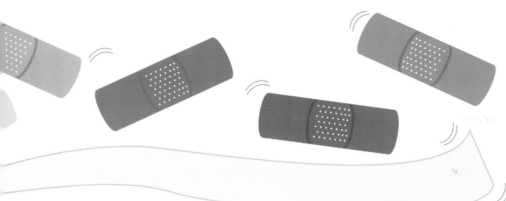

When You Have to Sneeze

(sung to the tune of "The Hokey-Pokey")

When you have to sneeze,
When you have to say, "Ah-choo!"
When you have to sneeze,
Please use a clean tissue.

You cover up your whole mouth
So you don't let germs get out.
That's what good health's about!

If There's a Fire

Teach youngsters this fire-smart song to heighten their awareness of fire safety. Then encourage your little ones to practice their stop, drop, and roll techniques.

(sung to the tune of "Five Little Ducks")

Brave firefighters always say,
"If there's a fire, stay away!
If fire's on you, then put it out!
Stop, drop, and roll!"
They always shout.

Street Smart

When you're walking home from school,
Remember these important rules:

When you want to cross the road,
Look left, then right before you go.

Never take a shortcut home.
Walk the path that you've been shown.

Don't talk to strangers you might meet,

But come straight home on your two feet!

Walk two fingers along leg.
Put index finger to temple.

Look left, then right.

Shake index finger.
*Walk two fingers
along other arm.*

*Shake index
finger.*
*Walk two fingers
in straight line.*

Health & Safety

Arthur's Boo-Boo Book

Read aloud *Arthur's Boo-Boo Book* by Marc Brown (Random House, Inc.) and have Doctor D. W. teach your youngsters what to do when someone gets hurt. After sharing the story, gather bandages and some antibacterial cream (or spray) for a lesson in basic first aid. Have a student volunteer pretend to have a cut on her finger. Review the steps from the book for proper boo-boo care. Have the child wash her hands, and then put a little cream and a bandage on her finger—followed by a kiss! Allow time for children to discuss past boo-boos they have had.

Then keep those bandages out for some more boo-boo fun that will strengthen youngsters' knowledge of body parts. Read aloud Shel Silverstein's poem "Band-aids" from *Where the Sidewalk Ends* (HarperCollins Children's Books). Then trace a child's body twice—once on each side of a length of bulletin board paper. Invite a volunteer to draw a face on one side. As you slowly reread the poem line by line, ask youngsters to place bandages on the outlined body in the same places that the boy is wearing them in the poem. (You'll need a total of 35 bandages.) Have older students count the bandages to find out how many boo-boos the poor boy has—or thinks he has!

I Am Fire

Share Jean Marzollo's *I Am Fire* (Cartwheel Books) to help little ones discover that fire can be both a friend and a foe. After reading the story, list all the ways fire can be useful, as well as ways that fire can get out of control. Then review this fire safety tip mentioned in the book: "If there is smoke, crawl under it. Stay low and go." Help youngsters practice this lifesaving technique with the help of this action poem.

If you see smoke in the air,
It's time to get out of there!
So get down low, low, low.
Crawl along, yes, go, go, go!
On your belly like a snake.
Stay really low, that's what it takes!
Crawl until you're out of there,
And you can breathe some fresh, clean air!

Look side to side.
Point to side with thumb.
Crouch down low, then lower.
Crawl on hands and knees.
Lie flat on belly.
Crawl on belly.
Crawl; then stand up.
Take a deep breath.

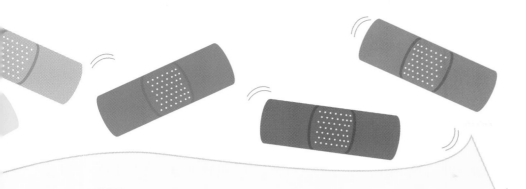

Dr. Kanner, Dentist With a Smile

Come along on a visit to a friendly dentist when you read *Dr. Kanner, Dentist With a Smile* (Children's Press) by Alice K. Flanagan. This story makes a wonderful introduction to a visit from a local dentist or dental hygienist. Explain to your students— just as Dr. Kanner does in the book—that your visitor also works hard to help people keep their teeth and gums healthy. Ask your visiting dental professional to show your youngsters the proper technique for tooth brushing. And after the visit, invite youngsters to make a special thank-you note for your visitor. Cut a sheet of white poster board into a large tooth shape. Program the cutout with a message similar to the one shown, and then invite all your little ones to sign it.

We don't want to brag, to boast, or to gush. But our teeth look GREAT since you showed us how to brush!
Thanks from Mrs. Flagg's class
Mary   Joe   Sam   Teena

Red, Yellow, Green...What Do Signs Mean?

Your youngsters are sure to show signs of interest as you read Joan Holub's *Red, Yellow, Green...What Do Signs Mean?* (Cartwheel Books). Before reading the story, place a small sticky note over each sign in the book. Distribute evenly the sign stickers provided in the book. As you read the story, ask each youngster to hold up his sticker when he sees or hears clues related to his sign in the text. If necessary, peel off the sticky note and have youngsters look at the sign sketch to find the matching sticker. As a fun extension of this story, take the children outdoors for a sign search. Walk through your school's or center's neighborhood looking for different kinds of signs, such as a stop sign, a school crossing sign, or a speed limit sign. Discuss the meaning of each sign you see.

Officer Buckle and Gloria

Your little ones will be barking for more as you culminate your health and safety unit with a reading of Peggy Rathmann's *Officer Buckle and Gloria* (The Putnam Publishing Group). After reading the book, read the safety tips provided inside the front and back covers of the book. Ask youngsters to review the tips they have learned from the book and from your study of health and safety. Write each tip mentioned on a construction paper star. Then divide your class into pairs and give each pair a star. Read the tip to the pair without the rest of the class listening. Then assign one child in each pair to play the part of Officer Buckle, and have the other child role-play Gloria. Direct "Gloria" to first demonstrate the tip on their star, and then have "Officer Buckle" recite the tip. Allow each pair time to practice before they perform their safety tip for the class. If desired, invite them to use props.

When it's time for the safety speech, challenge the class to guess the safety tip performed by each "Gloria" before "Officer Buckle" recites it. Later, post the tips around your classroom as star-studded safety reminders.

Nursery Rhymes

Jack and Jill's Opposites

Let Jack and Jill help your students fetch some knowledge of opposites. In advance, write each word from an opposite pair—such as *happy/sad, loud/quiet, fast/slow, hot/cold, dry/wet,* and *up/down*—on an index card, using a different color marker to write each pair. Back the cards with magnetic tape and display one word from each pair on your chalkboard or a magnet board. Then ask two children to play the parts of Jack and Jill. Give the pair a sand pail with one of the leftover cards inside. Have the pair skip along as the class sings this version of the traditional rhyme:

Jack and Jill went up the hill
To find a pair of opposites.
They found a card; it wasn't hard.
Now help them find its opposite!

Have Jack and Jill pull the card from their pail and show it to the group. Read the word to the students or ask a student volunteer to sound out the word. Then invite the group to find the word's opposite among the word cards on the board. Display the opposite pair together and use the ink color to check for accuracy. Then have a new Jack and Jill skip to the front of the group as you repeat the activity with a new pair of opposites.

Ps Porridge

Cook up this ABC version of porridge to strengthen students' letter recognition skills. Bring to group time a large metal pot, a supply of notepaper, a set of magnetic letters, and a class supply of pencils. Give each child a pencil and a few sheets of paper. Then place the letter *P* on the outside of the pot. Have youngsters identify the letter and then write it on a sheet of paper. Invite each child to drop his paper into the pot as you recite this rhyme. Invite a student volunteer to stir the *P*s porridge; then replace the magnetic *P* with another letter. Repeat the activity, this time using the name of the new letter in the chant.

[*Ps*] porridge hot,
[*Ps*] porridge cold,
[*Ps*] porridge in the pot
Nine days old.
Some like it hot,
Some like it cold,
Some like it in the pot
Nine days old.

Mary's Colorful Lambs

Recruit Mary's help in teaching colors to your little lambs. Title a bulletin board "Mary Had a Little Lamb; Its Fleece Was…" Label individual sentence strips with a color phrase to complete the sentence. For example, you might write "white as snow" on one strip and "green as grass" on another. Prepare a strip for each desired color; then staple each one to a different section of the bulletin board. Duplicate a class supply of the sheep pattern on page 201 on construction paper. Then cut out all the sheep. Place the cutouts in a center along with cotton balls, spring-type clothespins, and a paint color for each color mentioned on the display. Invite each center visitor to attach a clothespin to a cotton ball to make a paintbrush. Then have him paint his sheep the color of his choice. When the paint dries, help each child staple his sheep near the corresponding sentence strip on the display.

blue as the sky

"Hide-and-Sheep"

Use this fun small-group game to reinforce positional words and following directions. Copy, cut out, and laminate a construction paper sheep pattern (page 201). Appoint one child in the group to be Little Bo Peep and another child to be a shepherd. Give the shepherd a sheep cutout; then whisper into her ear a hiding place for the sheep. While Little Bo Peep covers her eyes, have the shepherd hide the sheep in the named place. Then invite Bo Peep to open her eyes and chant, "I'm Little Bo Peep. I've lost my sheep and don't know where to find it!" Have the shepherd answer Bo Peep with, "I'm a shepherd and this is what I've heard. Look [under a table]." Have the shepherd give a general clue regarding the location of the hidden sheep. Then encourage Little Bo Peep to search for the sheep until she finds it. Then play again with a new Bo Peep and shepherd until everyone has had a turn to both hide and find a sheep.

Yes, sir! Yes, sir! Four bags full!

Have You Any Wool?

Baa, baa, little sheep, have you any wool? Yes, sir! And in this woolly activity, youngsters will count out how many bags full. To make bags of wool, collect several cotton ball colors. Stuff ten snack-sized resealable plastic bags with the first cotton ball color. Repeat for the other colors. Seal each bag; then put the bags in a basket. Color one copy of the sheep pattern on page 201 to match each cotton color. Cut out the sheep, laminate them, and attach each one to a craft stick to make sheep puppets.

Give each puppet to a different volunteer. Lead the class in chanting, "Baa, baa, [color] sheep, have you any wool?" Encourage the child with the corresponding sheep to answer "Yes, sir! Yes, sir! [Number] bags full," inserting a number from one to ten in the blank. Then have him count out the corresponding bags of wool. Ask the class to count the bags together to check for accuracy; then have the child return the bags to the basket. Continue in this manner, giving each child a turn to be a sheep.

117

Nursery Rhymes

Mime-and-Rhyme Time

Set the stage for your little actors to give award-winning performances with this idea. Collect items to create nursery-rhyme prop boxes. For example, you might put a bowl, a spoon, and a plastic spider in a box labeled "Little Miss Muffet." Or mittens, cat-ear headbands, and a pie pan might be in a box for "Three Little Kittens." Place the boxes in a center; then use colored tape to mark off an area for a stage. Place a few chairs in front of the stage for the audience. Then invite small groups of youngsters to use the props to silently act out the nursery rhymes, while students in the audience try to identify the rhyme. After the correct rhyme is named, have the actors repeat their performance as the audience recites the rhyme. As you introduce each new rhyme, place a corresponding prop box in the center for more miming and rhyming fun.

"Hickory, dickory, dock!"

Rhymes in a Box

Use an accessory box to build nursery-rhyme activity in your block area. Fill the box with items to represent nursery rhymes of your choice. For example, put in a plastic sheep and play people to represent "Mary Had a Little Lamb," and a small stuffed mouse and a toy clock for "Hickory Dickory Dock." Then have youngsters build block structures to go along with the rhymes, such as Mary's schoolhouse or a tall grandfather clock. Invite children to use the props and the block structures to enhance their nursery-rhyme play.

My Own Nursery-Rhyme Book

Have youngsters create their own collection of traditional nursery rhymes with this activity. On separate sheets of paper, write or type the words to each rhyme learned during your nursery-rhyme unit. Duplicate a class supply of each rhyme. Then, after you introduce each rhyme to your class, place copies of that rhyme in the art center. Invite each child to the center to illustrate the rhyme. Collect the illustrations and save them in a file. At the end of your unit, collate and bind each child's drawings between tagboard covers. Have each youngster decorate his cover with nursery-rhyme stickers; then invite him to take his book home to enjoy some readin' and rhymin' with relatives.

Reciting Rhymes

Here's a way to get youngsters excited about listening to nursery rhymes. Tape-record individual children, each reciting or singing a favorite nursery rhyme. Place the tape at your listening center, along with a book of nursery rhymes. Invite youngsters to listen to each rhyme on the tape, then to find that rhyme in the nursery-rhyme book. For an additional challenge, ask youngsters to try to name the classmate who recites each rhyme.

Jack be nimble.
Jack be quick.
Jack jump over the candlestick.

Humpty Dumpty sat on a wall.

Humpty Dumpty had a great fall.

All the king's horses and all the king's men.

Couldn't put Humpty together again.

Line-by-Line Rhymes

Order up some rhyming fun with this prereading activity. Write the words to "Humpty Dumpty" or another nursery rhyme on chart paper. (If desired, use rebus pictures for younger children.) Write each line from the rhyme on a separate sentence strip. Display the complete rhyme in a center; then place the sentence strips near the rhyme. Ask youngsters to put the strips in order, using the chart as a guide. After the children have had success sequencing the sentence strips, cut the strips into short phrases or single words. Then invite all your king's men (and women) to put the rhyme together again!

Nursery Rhymes

Exciting Reciting

Spruce up Mother Goose with some varied voices! Recite rhymes using special voices, such as Old King Cole's majestic voice, Little Boy Blue's sleepy voice, and Mother Goose's elderly voice. Can the children think of other voices to use? Memorizing nursery rhymes has never been so much fun!

Rhyme Time

Help little ones identify rhyming words with this cloze activity. After youngsters have become familiar with a nursery rhyme, such as "Little Miss Muffet," stop before a selected rhyming word while reciting it. Then wait for the children to provide the missing word. For instance, you might say, "Little Miss Muffet sat on a…" Then stop to allow the class to say, "tuffet." Once the children have memorized the rhyme, say one line; then signal the class to supply the following line. Continue until the entire rhyme has been recited.

"Little Miss Muffet sat on a…"

"tuffet!"

Rhyme Review

A-tisket, a-tasket, a rhyme review in a basket! In a basket, collect items to represent the nursery rhymes you have studied, such as a plastic sheep for "Little Bo-Peep," a plastic egg for "Humpty Dumpty," and a candle for "Jack Be Nimble." Tell your little ones that Mother Goose left a basket to help them remember her rhymes. Then have one child at a time select an item from Mother Goose's basket. Help the child to identify the nursery rhyme that the item represents. Then have the child lead the class in reciting that rhyme.

"Jack be nimble..."

Name That Tune!

Try this nursery-rhyme version of Name That Tune. Many nursery rhymes such as "Mary Had a Little Lamb," "Baa, Baa, Black Sheep," and "Hickory, Dickory, Dock" have been set to music. Hum the tunes from these rhymes and others like them; then challenge your youngsters to identify the rhymes. After you've experimented with humming, lead little ones in clapping, snapping, or even tongue-clicking the rhythms of familiar rhymes. It's a rhythm-and-rhyme good time!

Reading Rhymes

Use nursery-rhyme collections to give your little ones some experience with context clues. Gather a few books that feature a collection of Mother Goose rhymes. As you slowly preview each book together, ask youngsters to carefully observe the illustrations. Challenge the class to identify each rhyme from the picture clues. Discuss the items that they recognize. If they have difficulty naming a rhyme, provide clues to assist them.
Lead the class in reciting each rhyme as it is identified.

"Look! The cat and the fiddle!"

Nursery Rhymes

The Royal Crown

Pay homage to the rhyming royalty, such as Old King Cole and the Queen of Hearts, by making a crown fit for a king or queen. To prepare, gather aluminum foil, sequins, shiny star stickers, gold or silver ribbon, a stapler, and glue. For each child, cut a simple crown from construction paper. Have each child cover his crown with aluminum foil. Then invite him to add star stickers, sequins, crumpled foil balls, and ribbon. When the glue dries, help the child fit the crown to his head; then staple the ends together. Provide him with a regal robe and scepter; then invite each imperial highness to role-play a royal nursery rhyme character.

Yummy in the Tummy!

Many nursery rhyme characters enjoy their fill of cake and pie. Commemorate the sweet eats of Mother Goose land with this play dough baking center. To begin, supply the play dough area with cake and pie pans, muffin tins, cupcake liners, and rolling pins or cylindrical wooden blocks. Add red and blue wooden beads to represent cherries and berries. Also include a few plastic sprigs of holly to top Little Jack Horner's Christmas pie, as well as 24 laminated black construction paper birds for a pie to set before the king. Then invite youngsters to mix in a dash of imagination and a pinch of appetite as they cook up a batch of nursery rhyme goodies. Yum! Yum!

Cottony Soft Sheep

Youngsters will ask to come "baa-ck" to this woolly activity time and time again. To make the frame of a sheep's body, a child clips two clothespins onto a craft stick, each about one-half inch from the end of the stick. She paints the clothespins and the craft stick with black paint. When the paint dries, she glues cotton batting to each side of the craft stick, leaving the ends uncovered to resemble the sheep's head and tail. Then she glues a wiggle eye to each side of the sheep's head. Invite your little shepherds to use their cottony soft sheep to act out "Mary Had a Little Lamb," "Baa, Baa, Black Sheep," or "Little Bo Peep."

Hurray for Rain!

"Rain, rain, go away." On second thought, invite the rain to stay—so your little puddle jumpers can collect some rain for play. On a day when "it's raining, it's pouring," provide each child with a sand pail, a cup, or another container in which to collect some rain. Once the rain stops, have each child fetch his container of water; then invite him to pour it into the water table. Discuss with the children how the rainwater might be similar to or different from tap water. Then add dishwashing liquid or bubble bath to the rainwater. Invite youngsters to use eggbeaters as well as other water toys in the soapy water. This fine-motor experience is bubbling over with fun!

Mother Goose Mice

Look who's on the loose—the mice from Mother Goose! Youngsters will squeak with delight when they make these mousy headbands. To make one, cut a triangle from a 6" x 9" piece of gray construction paper (as shown). Glue on two hole-reinforcement rings for eyes, a pink pom-pom nose, and black pipe-cleaner whiskers. Cut two gray circles and two smaller pink circles from construction paper; then glue them together to create ears. Glue the ears in place. Punch a hole (as shown) and add a gray pipe-cleaner tail. To make a headband, fit a 2" x 18" black construction paper strip around a child's head. Then staple the mouse in place so that the mouse's nose fits over the child's nose and the mouse's ears do not block the child's vision. Invite your little ones to wear their headbands as they recite "Three Blind Mice" or "Hickory Dickory Dock" in their sweet little mousy voices.

Humpty's Wall Had a Great Fall

See the "egg-citement" build as your little ones put together Humpty Dumpty's wall. To prepare, gather several cardboard bricks, a plastic egg from your housekeeping center, and a foam ball for every four children. (Empty boxes can be substituted for cardboard bricks.) Set these materials on a flat surface outdoors. Divide the class into four groups of king's men. Provide each group with one egg, one ball, and an equal number of bricks. Instruct the students in each group to use their bricks to cooperatively build Humpty Dumpty's wall, stacking rows of bricks on top of one another. When the walls are complete, place an egg on each wall to represent Humpty Dumpty. Then invite one child in each group to stand about six feet away from the wall. Give her a rubber ball to roll, and have her attempt to knock down the wall and Humpty. Have the group members rebuild their wall a few times, until all youngsters in the group have had a chance to knock it down. Thats what you call wall-to-wall fun!

Bo-Peep and Her Sheep

Help Little Bo-Peep find her sheep with this follow-the-leader activity. Designate one child to be Little Bo-Peep. Have the rest of the class pretend to be her herd of sheep. Ask them to scatter on the playground, as if she's lost them. Then give Little Bo-Peep a direction, such as, "Hop to the slide." As she follows your direction, she may tap any sheep she passes along the way. Those sheep then join her, performing the same movement. Once she arrives at her destination, give Bo-Peep another command, such as, "Gallop to the blacktop." Have her tap more sheep along the way. Continue until Bo-Peep and all her sheep are safely home (in a designated area). Play a few more times, so that other children get a chance to be Little Bo-Peep.

Jumpin' Jacks (and Jills)

Give your youngsters the opportunity to be nimble and quick! In advance, gather four candles and a large block of Styrofoam®. Cut the Styrofoam® block into four 3" x 3" pieces. Insert a candle into each Styrofoam® base. Then line up the candlesticks on an outdoor field, leaving four feet of space between adjacent candles. Ask your youngsters to form a line next to the first candle; then say the following rhyme as each child takes a turn jumping over the four candlesticks.

[Child's name], be nimble,
[Child's name], be quick,
[Child's name], jump over the candlesticks.

Along Came a Spider...

Get your little Miss (and Mister) Muffetts moving! Have children sit in a line, side by side. Draw or tape a parallel line several yards away from the line of children. Provide one child with a plastic spider ring or a black pom-pom (to represent a spider). Have this child walk back and forth behind the line of children as you all chant this version of the Mother Goose rhyme:

Little Miss Muffett sat on her tuffet,
Eating her curds and whey.
Along came a spider and sat down beside her,
And he made her [skip] away!

At the end of the verse, have the child holding the spider set it down next to one of the children in line. That child is then designated as Miss Muffett and must jump up and skip to the far line. After she reaches the line, she returns to the group and becomes the spider-holder for the next round. Announce a new movement—such as *run, hop, gallop,* or *stomp*—for the next Miss Muffett to perform.

Hickory, Dickory, Tick-Tock

Hickory, dickory, dock—it's time for a run up the clock! On a blacktop area or a sidewalk, use chalk to draw a long rectangle (9 to 12 feet long). Draw a circle inside the rectangle at one end, so that the drawing resembles a grandfather clock. Place a bell in the center of the circle. Then ask youngsters to form a line at the base of the clock. Announce a time (by the hour), and instruct your first little mouse to run to the top of the clock and ring the bell the corresponding number of times. Have him replace the bell and run back "down" the clock. Continue until every child has had a turn.

As a variation have the children run backward down the clock. Little ones are bound to enjoy every minute of this activity!

125

Nursery Rhymes

Hi, Humpty!

Ingredients:
1/2 hard-boiled egg per child
2 raisins per child
Hellmann's® Dijonnaise™
sweet relish
carrots

Utensils and Supplies:
1 plastic spoon per child
1 small paper cup per child
napkins
knife
vegetable peeler
grater
mixing bowl
tablespoon

Teacher Preparation:

Hard-boil one egg for every two children; then remove the shells. Cut each egg in half lengthwise. For each child, put the yolk from an egg half into a separate plastic cup. Peel and grate a large carrot. For every six eggs (12 servings), combine a mixture of 1 tablespoon relish, 2 tablespoons Dijonnaise™, and 1 tablespoon grated carrots. Peel a second carrot and slice it into rounds; then cut each carrot round in half. Arrange the ingredients and utensils near the step-by-step direction cards.

What to Do When the Snack Is Through

Use a leftover hard-boiled egg and a raw egg for an "eggs-traordinary" science experiment. Challenge youngsters to guess which egg is raw and which is cooked. Explain that you can tell the difference by spinning each egg. Tell students that if you stop each spinning egg with your finger, the hard-boiled egg will stop immediately, but the raw egg will keep moving a bit after you take your hand away. Try the experiment and ask youngsters to help you determine which egg is cooked and which is raw. Crack the eggs open to check.

(What happened? The cooked egg reacts to the motion as a solid object. But the liquid inside the raw egg continues to shift from the spinning, causing enough force to keep the egg moving.)

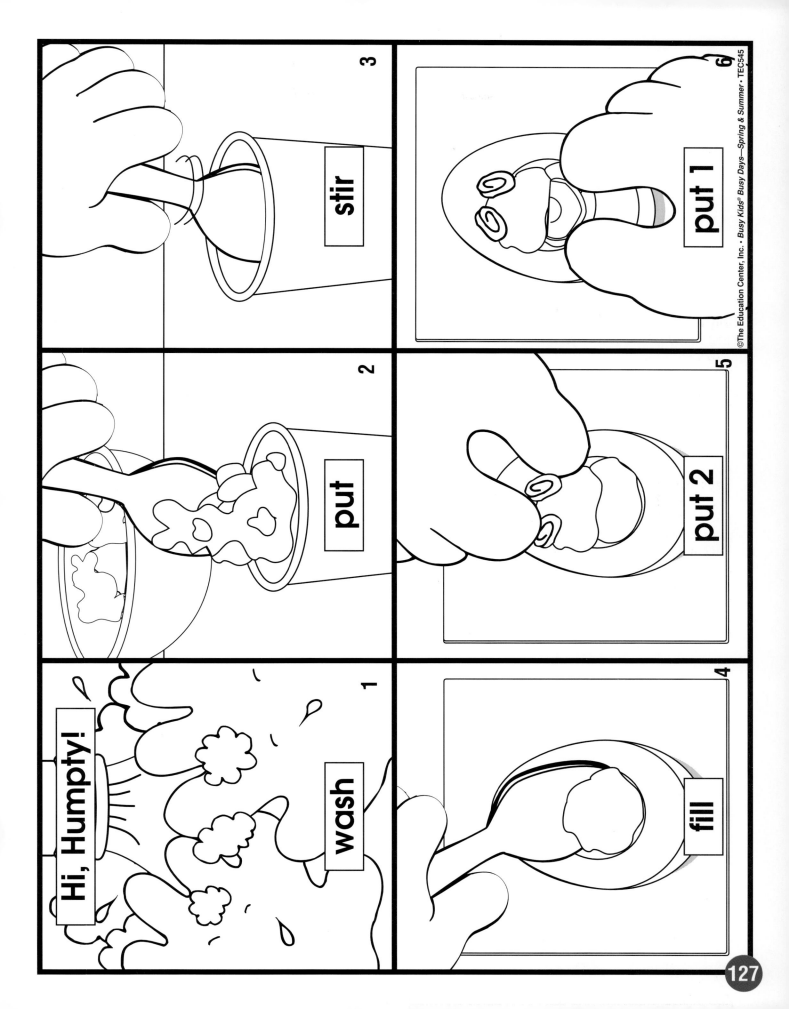

©The Education Center, Inc. • Busy Kids® Busy Days—Spring & Summer • TEC545

Nursery Rhymes

Mother Goose Clues

After singing this verse, give your little ones clues about a nursery rhyme. For example, you could give clues about "Jack and Jill" by saying, "This rhyme is about a boy and a girl," or "In this rhyme, someone falls down." Keep the clues going until a child guesses the rhyme. Then sing the song again and give clues about another rhyme. Once youngsters get the idea, invite them to make up the clues.

(sung to the tune of
"The Bear Went Over the Mountain")

I'm thinking of a nursery rhyme.
I'm thinking of a nursery rhyme.
I'm thinking of a nursery rhyme.
Oh, can you guess which one?

Where, Oh Where?

(sung to the tune of "Paw-Paw Patch")

Where, oh where, is [Little Bo Peep]?
Where, oh where, is [Little Bo Peep]?
Where, oh where, is [Little Bo Peep]?
[Looking around for her lost sheep.]

Invite youngsters to create additional verses by substituting characters and phrases such as the following for the underlined words:

Little Miss Muffet…Running far away from the spider.
Little Jack Horner…In a corner eating Christmas pie.
Humpty Dumpty…Sitting on top of a big, high wall.

Rhyme 'n' Rhythm

Here's a song to strengthen your youngsters' rhyming skills. After singing the song, ask students to recite the nursery rhyme mentioned. Then encourage them to identify the rhyming words in the rhyme.

(sung to the tune of "We Wish You a Merry Christmas")

Can you name the words that rhyme?
Can you name the words that rhyme?
Can you name the words that rhyme
In ["Little Bo Peep"]?

For further rhyming practice, substitute one of these nursery rhyme titles into the song:

"Little Boy Blue"
"Humpty Dumpty"
"Old King Cole"

I know! Cole and soul.

He stuck in his thumb...

Nursery Rhyme Time

Culminate your nursery rhyme unit by teaching this song to your class. Each time you repeat the song, name a different volunteer in the third line. Then invite that child to recite a nursery rhyme.

(sung to the tune of "Do You Know the Muffin Man?")

Oh, do you know a nursery rhyme,
A nursery rhyme, a nursery rhyme?
[Child's name] knows a nursery rhyme.
Please, share your rhyme with us.

Mary Had a Little Lamb

Share Bruce McMillan's charming photo-illustrated version of the classic *Mary Had a Little Lamb* by Sarah Josepha Hale (Scholastic Trade Books). Then invite each of your little animal lovers to describe a real or imaginary pet of his own. At the bottom of a sheet of paper, insert the child's name and pet into a sentence similar to the one shown. Have the child draw a picture of himself with his favorite animal friend above the sentence. (You might have younger children use magazine pictures of animals.) Invite each child to share his picture with the class as you read the text for this simple nursery rhyme adaptation.

[Wesley] had a [big elephant].
They loved each other so.
And everywhere that [Wesley] went
The [elephant] was sure to go.

After sharing each child's version of the nursery rhyme, bind the pages together for a class book that is sure to make your children laugh and play!

Wesley had a big elephant.

Big Fat Hen

"One, two, buckle my shoe." Come count to ten with the big fat hen and a coop full of chicks in Keith Baker's *Big Fat Hen* (Voyager Picture Books). Then pluck some feathers (from a craft-supply store) for this art activity. Set up your art center with paper, feathers, and a muffin tin of paints in varied colors. Encourage a child at this center to use a feather as a paintbrush to paint his entire paper. (Afterward, wash the feathers to be used again.) Once the paint dries, die-cut numerals from the feather paintings. (Or have older children use stencils to trace the numerals onto their feather paintings and then cut them out.) Reread the story slowly. As you say each number, encourage the children to hold up the matching numeral(s) that they have made. "Nine, ten, let's do it again!"

One !

Two !

To Market, to Market

Anna Miranda's hilarious twist to the familiar nursery rhyme *To Market, to Market* (Harcourt Brace) is sure to make your little ones laugh out loud! After reading the story, invite the class to make cabbage soup using ingredients from the story.

Cabbage Soup

1 baking potato
2 individual stalks of celery
1 beet (or small can of sliced beets)
2 large tomatoes
a handful of pea pods
   (or frozen snow pea pods)
1 bell pepper

1 garlic clove
half a cabbage
1 cup brown rice
4–6 carrots
1 onion
a handful of fresh or frozen okra
salt
pepper

Precut the vegetables into strips. Invite the children to use plastic knives to chop the potato, celery, beet, bell pepper, carrots, and okra into bite-size pieces. Chop the tomato, onion, and cabbage. Encourage the children to taste any vegetables that are new to them. Add the rice, garlic, and pea pods; then cover with water. Add salt and pepper to taste. Cook this hearty cabbage soup on medium heat until the potatoes and carrots are soft. "Yummity Yum!"

Hey Diddle Diddle & Other Mother Goose Rhymes

Add a little music to the rhythm and rhyme of Tomie dePaola's *Hey Diddle Diddle & Other Mother Goose Rhymes* (Paper Star). Choose rhymes from dePaola's collection that have a tune, such as "Baa, Baa, Black Sheep," "Hickory Dickory Dock," and "Rub-a-dub-dub." Use a kazoo to hum the tune before reading the rhyme. Can your youngsters guess the rhyme just by the tune? Give your little musicians some instruments, such as rhythm sticks and sand blocks. Distribute the different instruments evenly among your class. As you share one of the rhymes, encourage your little ones to play along while keeping the steady beat of the rhyme. Alternate instruments between verses or lines. Mother Goose has never sounded so good!

Little Lumpty

Your little ones will really crack up as you share the humor and whimsy of *Little Lumpty* by Miko Imai (Candlewick Press). As an "eggs-tension," set up Humpty's wall for those who are eager to experience it as Little Lumpty did. Place a row of cardboard blocks flat on the floor. (Or put a length of tape on the floor.) Invite a child to sit on the "wall" as you insert her name into the rhyme below. After chanting the rhyme together, listen to the giggles as the child pretends to fall from the wall just like Humpty and Lumpty.

[Courtney] Dumpty [sat] on the wall.
[Courtney] Dumpty had a great fall!

As a variation, try substituting other action words for *sat*, such as *walked, tiptoed, danced,* or *slept*.

Ocean

Colorful Sea Creatures

Strengthen color-word recognition and beginning sounds with the help of these underwater friends. Program each of six tagboard strips with "white whale," "red lobster," "gray dolphin," "black seal," "pink shrimp," or "yellow sea horse." Then duplicate the sea animal patterns on page 202 onto tagboard. Color each picture to correspond to its label on the strip; then cut the boxes apart. Copy the song shown onto chart paper; then display the song, phrases, and pictures during group time.

Tape a picture onto the blank in the first line of the song and the corresponding phrase onto the blank in the last line. As you sing the song to the tune of Raffi's "Baby Beluga," prompt students to name the animal in the first line and the color *and* animal in the last line. (You might encourage them to use initial sound clues, as well as the picture, to determine the color name.) Then change the prompts and sing the song again.

Baby _____ in the ocean blue,
How I wish I could swim with you,
In the kingdom of the deep blue sea,
With a little _____ next to me.

Baby  _____ in the ocean blue,

How I wish I could swim with you,

In the kingdom of the deep blue sea,

With a little ⎡ red lobster ⎤ next to me.

Pail 1

Name	Guess	Actual # of cups
Glenda	23	7
Kara	10	7
Charles	4	7
Dana	15	7
Caroline	11	7
Ben	9	7
Nick	8	7
Katie	6	7
Mitchell	12	7

Sand Pail Estimation

Little ones will have buckets of fun when they make estimates with sand! To prepare, label a small sand pail "1" and a larger pail "2." Then, for each pail, create a chart similar to the one shown. Place the pails and a measuring cup in your sand table. Ask each sand table visitor to write his name on both charts. Then have him estimate how many cups of sand are needed to fill each pail. (You might cover responses recorded by previous visitors.) Help the child record his estimates in the appropriate columns. Then instruct him to use the measuring cup to fill each pail. How many cups of sand were needed for the small pail? The large one? Have him write his findings on the chart. Then have the child compare his estimates to the actual numbers and to his classmates' results.

What "Shell" We Do?

Shell out some simple math skills with this beach time activity. Pour a layer of sand into each of several gift box bottoms. Add ten small shells to each box; then gather a small group of students and give each child a box-lid beach. Keep one mini beach for yourself. Depending on your students' ages and ability levels, try one of the following activities:

- Place your shells on the sand to form a shape. Have students copy the shape with their shells.
- Name a number and ask students to count out a corresponding number of shells.
- Arrange your shells into two sets. Ask youngsters to tell you if one set has more, fewer, or an equal number of shells. Then ask each child to arrange his shells into two sets for the group to compare.
- Tell simple math stories to your kindergartners, and have them use their shells to act them out. ("There were two shells on the beach. A wave washed up four more. How many are there all together?")

Ocean Waves

Your class will experience a wave of excitement over this fishy measurement activity. To prepare an ocean, use a permanent marker to draw waves of different lengths on a gallon-sized resealable plastic bag (as shown). Draw a fish outline at the end of each wave. Pour two cups of water into the bag; then add a few drops of blue food coloring. Slowly zip the bag, releasing all the air from it. Then seal the zipped edge with wide packing tape for extra security against leaks. Place the ocean bag in a center along with some Goldfish® tiny crackers and a wipe-off marker. To use, measure each wave with crackers. Count the crackers and record the corresponding numeral on the fish at the end of the wave. Count the crackers again for accuracy; then erase the numerals with a damp paper towel. After each child's turn, invite her to snack on her fish crackers. It's time to catch a wave!

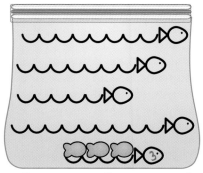

Gone Fishin'

Fishing for a way to get youngsters excited about learning letters? Then invite them on this fishing expedition! Cut a pair of fish from craft foam for each letter of the alphabet. Use a permanent marker to program pairs of fish with corresponding uppercase and lowercase letters. Put the fish in your water table along with fish or butterfly nets. Tape a short length of yarn—or fishing line—to the table for each fish pair. Tie a clothespin to the loose end of each line. Then invite each water table visitor to fish for pairs of matching fish with a net. Have him clip each pair to the end of a fishing line to display the catch of the day. It's a letter-perfect day for fishing!

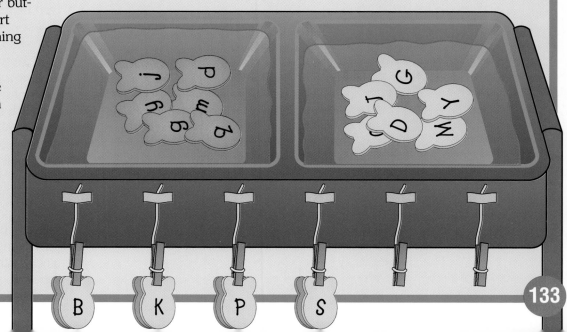

133

Ocean

Down by the Sea

Youngsters will be more than willing to dive into this alluring book-and-beach center. To prepare, fill the shelves of your reading center with books about the beach or ocean. Adorn the walls of the center with fishnets and sea-life posters. Add that seaside feeling with items such as a beach umbrella (you might sink the umbrella handle into a large, heavy clay pot of plaster of paris), a beach chair, some floats, and a beach bag containing an empty bottle of sunscreen, sun visors, sunglasses, flip-flops, goggles, and a beach towel. If desired, also add a small kiddie pool. Then place a tape recorder and a tape of beach sounds in the center. Then invite youngsters to soak up a few rays while engaging in some sizzlin'-hot summer reading at the beach.

Collecting Seashells

Your little ones will be as happy as clams with this counting activity. To prepare, make a tagboard tracer of the sand-pail pattern on page 203. (You don't need the fish pattern for this activity.) Use a black permanent marker to trace the pattern several times onto a Formica® tabletop, adding the handle detail. (Or make tagboard sand pails, laminate them, and tape them to a table in your math center.) Use the permanent marker to program each pail with a numeral from 1 to 10. Put a real sand pail full of seashells on the table. Then encourage your little shell seekers to count out the number of shells corresponding to the numeral on each sand pail. For variety, change the numerals on the pails each day. To erase the sand pails, simply wash the table with alcohol; then gently scrub away any remaining stains with Comet®. Only the learning will be permanent!

Sea Sights and Sounds

This imaginary seaside expedition is bound to reel youngsters into your discovery center. Gather ocean-related items, such as an assortment of shells, starfish, sharks' teeth, seagull feathers, sea horses, coral, and seaweed. If possible, add a crab or lobster shell to the collection. (You might request these from the seafood department of your grocery store.) Fill the top of a large, deep gift box with a layer of sand. Place the sea items in the sand along with a magnifying glass. Then invite youngsters to discover the treasures of the sea.

Oceans of Bubbles

Are you fishing for a project to make your youngsters bubble over with enthusiasm? Then try this seaworthy project in your art area. In advance, use the fish pattern on page 203 to cut a few fish shapes from thin craft sponge. In your art center, set out cookie sheets, cups of bubble solution, straws, blue food coloring, half-sheets of white construction paper, the fish-shaped sponges, and shallow trays of tempera paint. Each child who visits the center first writes his name on a half-sheet of paper. He then places a cup of bubble solution atop a cookie sheet. He adds 10–12 drops of blue food coloring to his cup, then uses a straw to blow bubbles in his cup until they rise above the rim. He places his personalized piece of paper on top of the cup to capture the bubble prints, then sets his paper aside to dry. He may revisit the center later to make fish-shaped sponge prints on the bubbly water background.

Ships Ahoy!

Invite each of your little sailors to captain his very own boat at the water table. Put a box of LEGO® or DUPLO® blocks near the water table along with some DUPLO® people. Encourage the children to put the building blocks together to make their own floating vessels. Encourage them to man their ships with toy people posing as ship captains, fishermen, or passengers. Then challenge each youngster to brainstorm ways to sail his boat from one end of the water table to the other without touching the boat. A child might suggest that he blow his boat across the water or create waves to push his boat across. Invite him to try out some of his ideas. It's plain to "sea" that creativity will be afloat at this center!

135

Ocean

Is it a shovel?

Something's Fishy!
Fishing for a new way to build vocabulary? Then dive right into this descriptive activity. In advance, collect several beach items, such as a pair of sunglasses, a bottle of sunblock, or a sand pail and shovel. Put one of these items in a beach bag. During circle time, describe the item that is inside the bag and ask youngsters to guess what object you are describing. Continue to play this guessing game by changing the item inside the bag. In the days that follow, invite each child to bring to school a beach item of his choice to place in the mystery bag. Then help him provide clues to help the class name the mystery object.

Songs by the Seashore
Use this seaworthy song to strengthen prereading skills. To prepare, copy the words of the song below on chart paper. Then gather pictures of ocean-related items, such as a shell, a dolphin, or a starfish. Invite a youngster to select a picture; then hold the picture over the blanks on the chart to complete each line of the song. To shovel up some added fun, use a sand shovel to point to the words as you sing along.

Bring It Back!
(sung to the tune of "My Bonnie Lies Over the Ocean")

My ____ lies under the ocean.
My ____ lies under the sea.
My ____ lies under the ocean.
Oh! Bring back my ____ to me.

(Optional)
Bring back! Bring back!
Oh! Bring back my ____ to me, to me.
Bring back! Bring back!
Oh! Bring back my ____ to me.

Hmm, I think it's a shark!

Famished Fish

Create commotion by the ocean as you take a bite out of subtraction with this countdown rhyme. As you recite the rhyme, have little ones use their fingers to symbolize each number of fish.

Out in the middle of the ocean so
     deep,
[Five] little fish swim and leap.
Along comes a shark…
GULP!

(Continue to repeat the first verse using four little fish, three little fish, and two little fish. Then end the rhyme with the verse that follows.)

Out in the middle of the ocean so
     deep,
One little fish started to weep.
Along came a shark
And said, "I'm full!"

Follow up the fingerplay with this variation. Give each child five Goldfish® crackers to use as manipulatives. As you recite the rhyme again, have each little shark feed on a fish each time he says, "GULP!"

Sock It to 'Em!

Put your little beachcombers' senses to the test with this activity. In advance, collect pairs of shells similar in shape and size or pairs of rubber sea creatures, such as fish, crabs, or sharks. Have your youngsters sit in a circle; then place one item from each pair of objects in the center. Pass the remaining items for the children to see and touch; then collect them. Without the children seeing, place one of these items inside a sock. Tie a loose knot in the end of the sock, and then pass it around the circle. Ask each child to describe how the hidden object feels. Next, challenge youngsters to point to the object in the center of the circle that matches the item in the sock.

"Sea-sational" Graphing

The loose ends of your ocean unit will be "tide" together with this graphing activity. Draw a simple bar graph on poster board. If desired, scallop the top of the poster board to resemble waves. Ask each child to name her favorite sea creature. At the bottom of the graph, make a simple drawing of each type of ocean animal named. Provide small photographs of each child or small sticky notes labeled with each child's name to use as graph markers. Have each child place her photo or sticky note above her favorite sea animal. Now your youngsters' ocean favorites will not be forgotten!

137

Ocean

Clip and Catch

This deep-sea fishing activity is sure to lure your little seafarers to the water table. To prepare, cut a supply of simple fish shapes from sheets of craft sponge. Have your children watch as you place the sponge cutouts in the water table; then invite their comments as the sponges expand. Encourage youngsters to visit this center to "fish" using spring-type clothespins. If desired, set an egg timer; then challenge students to catch as many fish as possible within the designated time. This will be a fishing expedition to remember!

The Odd Octopus

What do your youngsters know about this odd sea creature called the octopus? Hold a class discussion to find out; then show students some photos of real octopi to add to their knowledge. After establishing that the octopus has a round body, two big eyes, and eight long arms, tell your class that it also has round suckers on each arm. The suckers help the octopus to move across the ocean floor and to grab small animals to eat. After your discussion, invite each child to make her own octopus with this idea.

To make an octopus body, a child cuts a large circle from her choice of construction paper colors. Then she cuts or tears eight strips of paper for the octopus's arms. She glues her octopus together on a sheet of blue construction paper; then she glues two construction paper eyes onto her octopus. To replicate the octopus's suckers, she peels and sticks several hole reinforcements on each of its eight legs. Encourage each child to share her octopus creation and knowledge with her family.

Star of the Seashore

Fine-motor practice is the star of this activity! To prepare, draw a starfish shape on a sheet of colorful construction paper for each child. Show a picture of a real starfish to your students and explain that the undersides of starfish are covered with suction disks that they use for crawling and obtaining food. Then invite each child to create his own starfish. To begin, have him cut out a starfish from his choice of colored paper. Ask him to dip pieces of Froot Loops® cereal into glue; then have him stick the cereal to his starfish to represent suction disks. After the glue dries, display all the starfish on a bulletin board covered with blue background paper.

Sifting Sand

Your little beachcombers will enjoy sifting their way through this "sand-sational" activity. Invite each child to make a sand sieve from a disposable aluminum pan. Simply place the pan on a thick layer of newspaper. Supervise as a child uses a nail to poke a number of small holes in the bottom of the pan. Then invite the child to use her sieve in your sand table, along with a collection of scoops, shells, and pails.

Sea Station

When youngsters visit this station, you'll "sea" their fine-motor skills rise to a new level! To prepare, use a permanent marker to draw a line around the middle of each of several small, clear plastic cups. Partially fill a few larger plastic cups with water; then add a few drops of blue food coloring to make "seawater." Then place a cup of water, a small plastic cup, and a straw in each of several shallow containers. Put the containers in a center.

Show one group of youngsters at a time how to transfer the seawater from a larger cup to a smaller cup by using a straw. To do this, simply slip a straw into a large cup; then cap the straw tightly with your index finger to hold the water inside. Lift the finger-capped straw out of the water and place it in a small cup. Then remove your finger to release the water into the cup. Invite each child to transfer water into her cup in the same manner. Have her repeat the process until she fills her cup to the line. Then have her pour the water back into the large cup for the next sea adventurer.

139

Ocean

Seashells by the Shore

Have your little beachcombers dig their toes into wet sand for a "sense-ational" experience! In an outdoor area, fill a dishpan or large plastic storage container with water. Add sand and smooth, clamlike seashells to the water. Place a towel and a child's chair next to the container. Then invite one child to take off his shoes. Have him sit in the chair and place his feet in the water. Challenge him to pick up the shells with his toes and place them on the ground. Once he has grabbed a few shells with his toes, have him count the shells and return them to the container for the next shell collector. Use the towel to dry wet feet. Splish! Splash! A "toe-tal" blast!

Beach-Ball Volleyball

Surf up some fun with Beach-Ball Volleyball! In an outdoor area, position two chairs six feet apart. Tie one end of a long rope to the back of each chair. Tie ribbons or crepe paper streamers onto the rope. Divide the class into two groups; then have the members of each group sit cross-legged on opposite sides of the rope. Have the children throw a beach ball over the rope and catch it. What a way to keep your youngsters on the ball!

Gone Fishin'!

Something fishy will be going on in your classroom when your little ones dive and jump to this sea-drenched song. As you sing the song, encourage your little fish to act out the words "jump," "dive," and "swim." Wow! What a school of fish!

Fish Swim
(sung to the tune of "My Bonnie Lies Over the Ocean")

A fish swims around in the ocean.
A fish jumps and dives in the sea.
A fish swims around in the ocean.
He jumps and he dives merrily.

Fish jump! Fish dive!
Fish swim around in the sea, the
  sea.
Fish jump! Fish dive!
Fish swim around in the sea.

Jumpin' Jellyfish

Watch your youngsters get stung by jellyfish fever! First have each child make his own jellyfish. To make one, cut a paper plate in half. Along the straight edge of one-half of the paper plate, glue colorful crepe paper streamers. Then staple the two halves of the plate together. Have your little ones swish and sway their jellyfish streamers in the outside air, like jellyfish swish through water. Encourage youngsters to hold the jellyfish high with streamers flapping through the air as they jump, twirl, and leap. Swish, swish, swish go the jellyfish!

Commotion by the Ocean

Watch your outdoor play area become a vast ocean awash with "sea-sational" underwater creatures. To prepare, cut out large sea-animal shapes—such as starfish, sharks, and whales—from poster board. Invite your children outside to a concrete or blacktop area. Ask youngsters to use colored chalk to trace the sea-animal shapes. Encourage the children to use large arm motions to color and add features to the sea creatures. Add large wavy surf lines. Have youngsters run along the path of the surf lines, then pretend to dive in and swim around the creatures.

Ocean

Sand Pail

Ingredients:
1/3 cup prepared instant vanilla pudding per child
3 vanilla wafers per child
string licorice
shell candy (optional)

Utensils and Supplies:
1 zippered plastic bag per child   1/3-cup measuring cup
one 5-oz. paper cup per child   large mixing bowl
1 plastic spoon per child   knife

Teacher Preparation:
  In a large bowl, make the pudding according to package directions. Punch two opposing holes at the top of each paper cup. Cut the string licorice so that you have a nine-inch length for each child. Arrange the ingredients and utensils near the step-by-step direction cards. If desired, purchase shell candy from a specialty candy store, and have students add a few pieces to their finished sand pails.

What to Do When the Snack Is Through

  Use extra vanilla pudding for pudding painting. Encourage each child to fingerpaint her name, shapes, or sea creatures. Make cookie crumbs from any leftover vanilla wafers; then place the crumbs on a cookie sheet. As each child finishes painting, encourage her to press her pudding-covered hands in the cookie crumbs to make her hands "sandy." Then invite her to lick the sand right off her hands. Mmm, tasty!

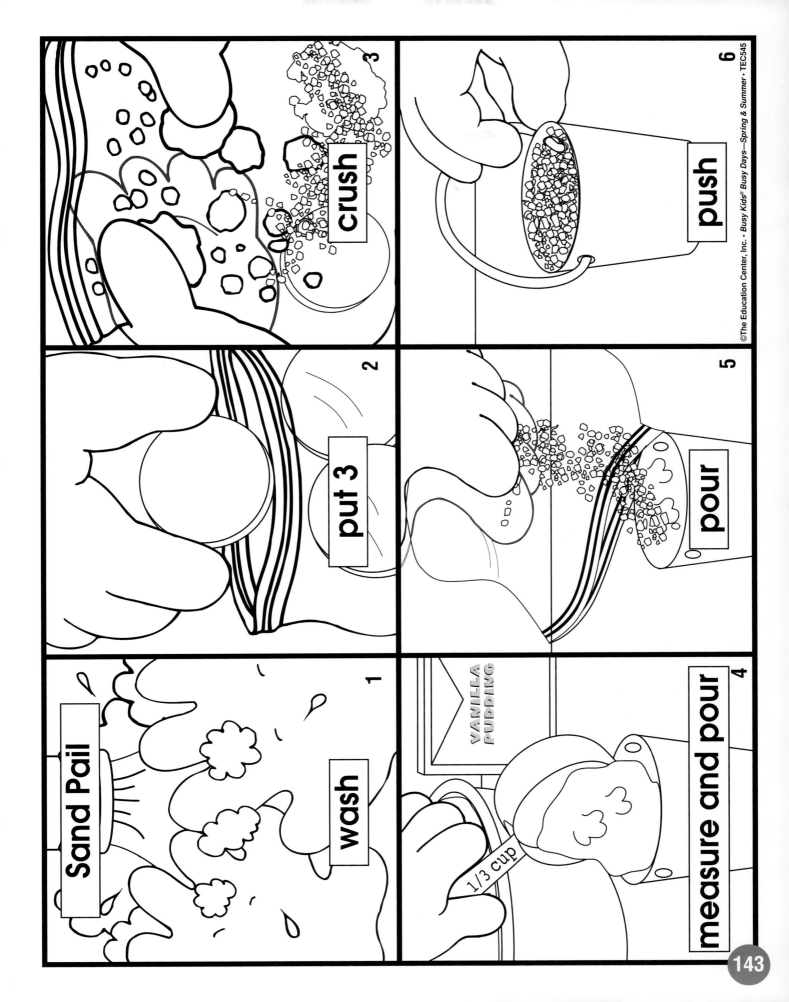

crush **3**

push **6**

put 3 **2**

pour **5**

Sand Pail wash **1**

VANILLA PUDDING

1/3 cup

measure and pour **4**

Ocean

Colorful Fish

Fishin' for a song about our fish friends? Then teach this seaworthy tune to your little guppies. If desired, have each youngster make a stuffed fish to swim along to the song. To make one, cut out two identical, large, construction paper fish. Staple the fish together back-to-back, leaving the bottom edges open. Then color each side of the fish in a similar manner. Paint over the crayon designs with diluted blue tempera paint. Once the paint dries, stuff the fish with crumpled pieces of scrap paper. Then staple the bottom edges together for a ready-to-swish fish. After swimming the stuffed fish along to this song, hang them from the ceiling to create a colorful display.

(sung to the tune of "Down in the Valley")

Down in the ocean,
The ocean so blue,
There are many fishes,
Red, green, pink, and blue.
Some come with stripes
   and polka dots, too!
Down in the ocean,
The ocean so blue!

The Deep Blue Sea

Set your youngsters' sights on the sea with this seafaring song. Ask each child to name something she might see at the beach, such as dolphins or sand crabs. Then insert her name and response in the song.

(sung to the tune of "A Sailor Went to Sea, Sea, Sea")

[Child's name] went to the sea,
   sea, sea,
To see what [she] could see,
   see, see.
And all that [she] did see, see, see,
Were [seashells] in the sea,
   sea, sea.

My Beach Bag

Youngsters will find this activity a fun challenge! In advance, hide several sand toys and a beach bag around the classroom. Then sing the first two verses of this song using a forlorn voice. Ask youngsters to help you find the missing beach items. (If necessary, give students clues to help them find the items.) Once the items are gathered and placed in the bag, joyously sing the last verse.

(sung to the tune of "A-Tisket, A-Tasket")

My beach bag, my beach bag,
My filled-with-toys beach bag—
Was on my way to the shore today,
And on the way I lost it.

I lost it. I lost it.
Yes, on the way I lost it.
With all my castle-building toys,
Oh, I'm so sad I lost it.

We found it! We found it!
Yes, finally we found it!
With all my castle-building toys,
Oh, I'm so glad we found it!

Going to the Ocean

(sung to the tune of "I've Been Working on the Railroad")

I am going to the ocean,
To the ocean blue.
I am going to the ocean,
And you can come along, too.
We could watch the big and blue waves
Rising up and rolling down.
We could look for pretty seashells
On the sandy ground.

Come along with me.
Come along with me.
Come along with me to the deep blue sea.
Come along with me.
Come along with me.
Come along with me today.

145

Ocean

> That's a star!

At the Beach

Get your little bathing beauties ready for a trip to the beach. Before reading *At the Beach* by Anne and Harlow Rockwell (Aladdin Paperbacks), pack a beach bag with items you might take to the beach, such as sunglasses, sunscreen, a pail, a shovel, a towel, a book, a juice box, and a bag of pretzels. Make sure you have one item in the bag for each child. After enjoying the story together, tell the class you are going on an imaginary trip to the beach. Pass the beach bag around your group as they sit in a circle, and have each child select one item to hold. Next, recite the following poem:

Let's go to the beach.
Let's pack up right away.
Let's bring everything we need
For the perfect beach day.

Now give a child the empty beach bag and have her say, "I will pack [item]." She then places her object in the bag and passes it to the next child. That child says, "I will pack [the previous item] and [his item]," as he puts his item in the bag. Continue in this manner until every child has had a turn. Encourage youngsters to name the items in the same order as they were placed in the bag. If a child has difficulty remembering the items, solicit help from the class.

> I will pack the sunscreen.

Sea Shapes

Youngsters will dive right into shape recognition when you read *Sea Shapes* by Suse MacDonald (Voyager Picture Books). Before sharing the story, cut a length of blue bulletin board paper to make a mural. From various colors of construction paper, cut a desired number of each shape featured in the story. Give one shape to each child prior to reading. As you turn each page, have youngsters with the matching shape hold it up and name the shape. Then give them ample time to find the shapes in each picture. Afterward, invite each child to paste his shape to the bulletin board paper before using markers to turn it into a sea creature of his own. To embellish the sea creatures and seascape, provide wiggle eyes, sticky dots, and crepe paper streamers. As a finishing touch, use blue watercolor paint to add wavy lines to this ocean so blue.

Out of the Ocean

Sun, sand, and surf—the beach has much to offer. Read *Out of the Ocean* by Debra Frasier (Harcourt Brace & Company) and you'll feel like you're really there! Set up this beach treasure hunt to reinforce the book's message that there are wonderful treasures wherever you look. Gather ocean-related items—such as an assortment of shells, sea glass, seagull feathers, and coral—and hide the items in your outdoor sandbox. (You can find ocean objects at craft stores or aquariums.) Ask each child to bring a beach towel and sunglasses to school. After reading this beautifully illustrated story, grab your beach towels and head for the sun and the sand (the sandbox). Invite a few children at a time to search "the beach" for ocean treasures. Once a treasure is found, have the child bring it back to his towel to examine it. Invite your little beachcombers to exchange treasures. Remind youngsters to remember to look for treasures wherever they go!

Lottie's New Beach Towel

Count on Lottie from *Lottie's New Beach Towel* by Petra Mathers (Atheneum) to inspire your children to dream up lots of new ideas. After reading the book, discuss the clever ways Lottie used her beach towel in the story. Challenge your children to be as ingenious as Lottie. Gather a class supply of scrap materials, each measuring at least six inches square. Give each child one piece and ask her to think of different ways she could use it. Could it be used in a game? Could it be part of a picture? Could it be worn in some way? Give the children enough time to brainstorm; then marvel at their creativity as they share their ingenious ideas with one another.

Swimmy

Are you fishin' for the ideal story to teach your youngsters about the importance of teamwork? Then read aloud *Swimmy* by Leo Lionni (Alfred A. Knopf, Inc.). As an extension, invite your class to work as a team to make a giant fish similar to the one in the story. Set up a painting station with a length of blue bulletin board paper, red and black tempera paint in separate shallow pans, and a black marker. On the paper, lightly pencil in the shape of a giant fish. Ask a child to press one hand into the black paint; then have him hold his fingers together and press his hand onto the fish outline where the eye should be. Have the remaining children make one or more similar handprints—in red—until the fish outline is filled in. Once the paint is dry, invite each child to use the marker to add an eye to her red fish. Add a wiggle eye to further distinguish the black Swimmy. Mount the finished project on a bulletin board to show off your class's terrific teamwork!

Space

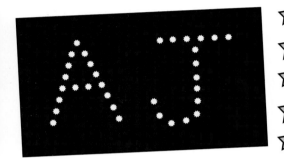

It's in the Stars

Your little stars will sparkle with delight when they create these star-studded name posters. To prepare, write each child's name in large letters on a sheet of white construction paper. Back each page with black construction paper; then staple the corners of the pages together. To make a poster, ask each child to position her paper over a large piece of cardboard or a folded towel. Have her use a pushpin to make closely spaced holes along the lines of each letter. (Children may want to complete this task over a few work sessions, especially if they have longer names.) Then help her carefully separate the two pages. Invite the child to hold her black page up to the light. The tiny holes will look like stars that spell out her name! Display the name posters in a window to show off your stars to the world.

Shapely Rockets

These rockets are loaded with opportunities for following directions and recognizing shapes. In advance, cut out a supply of squares, rectangles, and triangles from various colors of construction paper. Place the shapes on a table, along with sheets of black construction paper, glue sticks, glitter, and star stickers. Then invite one small group at a time to create rockets as students listen to the directions below. After each child builds his rocket, invite him to decorate the sky surrounding it with his choice of glitter or star stickers.

—Find a square. Glue it to the bottom of the paper.
—Find a rectangle. Glue it on top of the square.
—Find a triangle. Glue it on top of the rectangle.

Sun Prints

Shine some light on your youngsters' name and letter recognition skills with this sunny activity. On a bright, sunny morning, give each child letter cutouts to spell his first (or last) name. Help him back each letter with a piece of rolled tape; then have him tape his letters onto a sheet of construction paper to spell his name. Place the papers outside in direct sunlight for several hours. Then have each child carefully remove the letters from his paper. What did he discover? Explain that the parts of the paper exposed to the sun faded, but the areas covered by the letters were protected from the light and did not fade. Children will be amazed at the power of the sun!

Earth Circles Round the Sun

Teach youngsters this space-related chant to reinforce the days of the week.

Earth circles round the sun
One time every day.
Sunup, sundown.
That's what we know.
Time to sleep and play.

Circle one hand around the other.
Hold up one finger.
Raise hands up and down.

Rest head on hands. Open eyes and smile.

Monday, Tuesday,
Wednesday, Thursday,

Slap thighs; then clap hands.
Slap thighs; then clap hands.

Friday, Saturday,
Sunday.

Slap thighs; then clap hands.
Slap thighs.

Far Out!

Bring the concept of ordinal numbers closer to home with this solar system activity. To begin, label each of nine paper plates with a different planet name. Label a yellow paper plate "Sun."

During a group time, explain that the nine planets in our solar system move around the sun and each one is a different distance away from the sun. Ask a student to hold the yellow paper plate and stand in front of the group to represent the sun. Then give the plate labeled "Mercury" to another child and ask him to stand next to the sun. Explain that Mercury is *first* in line next to the sun. Continue with the remaining eight planets, naming each one and discussing its order in line from the sun. Then invite student volunteers to answer as you pose questions, such as "Which planet is *third* from the sun? Which planet is *fifth*?" Repeat this space expedition until ordinal numbers and the planets are less alien to your little space travelers.

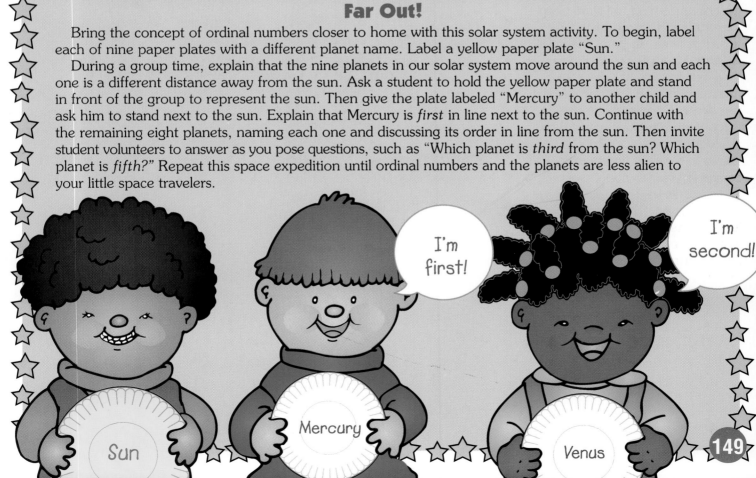

Space

Stick With the Stars

★ ★ ★ ★ ★

5

Before your intergalactic explorers take off for the moon, they'll need to practice the countdown to liftoff with this center activity. Program each of ten wide craft sticks with a different number of foil stars from one to ten. To prevent the stars from peeling off, paint the craft sticks with a light coat of clear fingernail polish. Then use a permanent marker to program each of ten additional craft sticks with a numeral from 1 to 10. Place both sets of craft sticks in a center. Invite each space traveler to match each star stick to its corresponding numeral stick. Then challenge youngsters to sequence the sticks in reverse order from ten to one. Ready? Ten, nine, eight…

Let's Visit the Planetarium!

Launch into space exploration with your own planetarium, made from a refrigerator box. If desired, enlist the help of your students to paint the exterior of the box black. After the paint dries, remove one end of the box. Have youngsters crawl inside and attach glow-in-the-dark stars to the interior of the box. Then invite them to use glow-in-the-dark crayons to create their own stars and planets on the inside and outside of the box. Cut a flap large enough to crawl through at the cutaway end of the box. Stand the box on its cutaway end, and have one space explorer at a time visit the planetarium to view the stars and planets. After each child's visit, have him use glow-in-the-dark crayons to draw his observations on black construction paper. Your youngsters will be starstruck in this center!

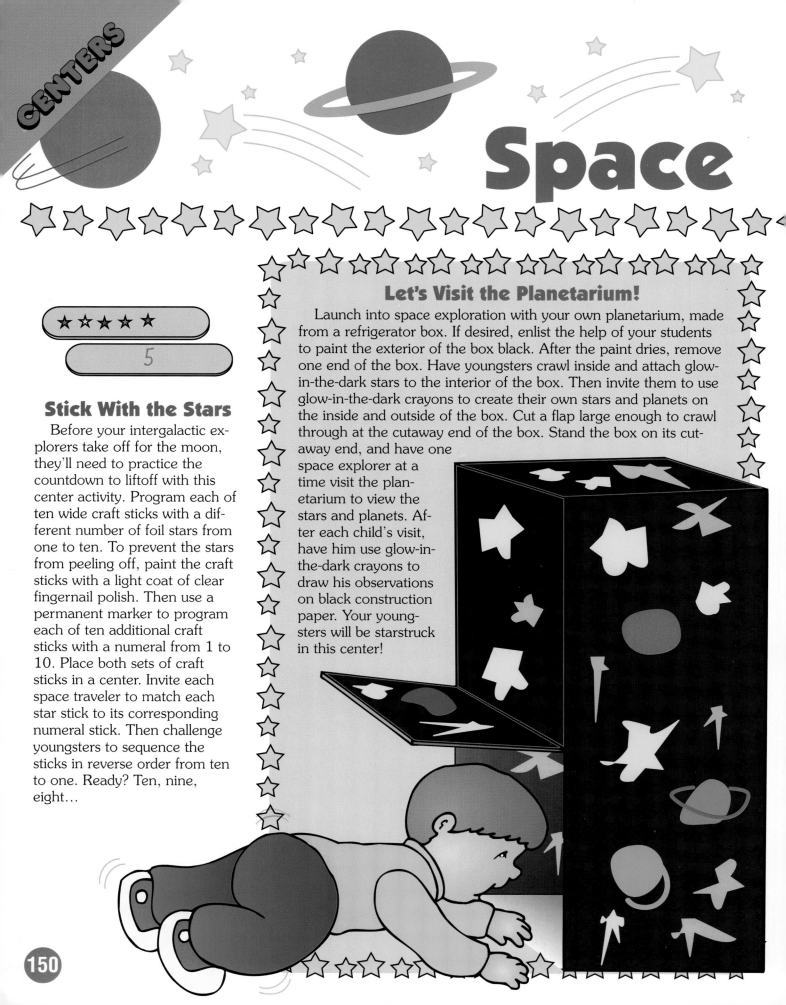

Star Light, Moon Bright

Invite your young stargazers to create their own starry-night pictures with this art-center activity. Supply the center with 12" x 18" sheets of black construction paper, small paper plates, and star stickers. Also add glue, paintbrushes, and a glitter-paint mixture of yellow paint and gold or iridescent glitter. When a child visits this center, she creates a moon by painting a paper plate with the glitter paint. When the paint dries, she glues her moon to a sheet of black construction paper; then she adds star stickers to the paper. Display the finished night-sky creations on your classroom ceiling to create a glorious galaxy.

Journey Into Outer Space

Watch your youngsters' enthusiasm rocket sky-high at this sensory table. To prepare, lay a sheet of bubble wrap under a layer of sand in your sand table. Then add Styrofoam® materials, such as packing pieces, balls of different sizes, and cups or bowls. Provide pipe cleaners and straws cut into different lengths. Then invite youngsters to use their imaginations—and the provided materials—to create everything from spaceships and planets to aliens and flying saucers.

Space: The Final "Fun-tier"

Dress up your dramatic-play center for imaginary explorations into space. To prepare, provide dress-up items to represent articles that an astronaut might wear, such as an oversized gray sweat suit, heavy work gloves, adult's rubber boots, a headset from your listening center, goggles, and a bike helmet. Then invite your little space travelers to suit up and take off on an imaginary space adventure!

Space

Circle-Time Countdown

Give your future astronauts some practice with counting backward. Explain to the children that when a spaceship is ready to be launched, the people at mission control count backward as they confirm that everything is working properly. Use your fingers to demonstrate how to count down from ten; then have students echo you and copy your finger movements. After the children have had plenty of practice counting backward, display numeral flash cards with numerals from 1 to 10. Ask a volunteer to identify the numeral on a designated card; then have him lead the class in the countdown. For example, if the numeral on the card is 6, have the children stand and count, "6-5-4-3-2-1—Blastoff!" Encourage youngsters to jump high each time they complete their countdown.

A Twinkling Tune

Give your little space travelers a review of our solar system with this twinkling tune. Encourage the children to create additional verses of their own.

A Solar System Song
(sung to the tune of "He's Got the Whole World in His Hands")

We've got [the solar system] in our sights.
We've got [the solar system] in our sights.
We've got [the solar system] in our sights.
We've got [the solar system] in our sights.

We've got the golden sun…

We've got the twinkling stars…

We've got Pluto and Mars…

Space Exploration

Have your little astronauts suit up for a simulated space flight to the moon. Encourage students to use their imaginations as you lead them in the following dramatization. First, pretend to put on space suits. Enter the spaceship and fasten seat belts. Push the lever to start the engines. Count down, "10-9-8-7-6-5-4-3-2-1—Blastoff!" As you enter outer space, steer the spaceship to the left, to the right, and then straight ahead. Turn quickly to miss a meteor. As you approach the moon, release the landing gear and gently land. Unbuckle seat belts and exit the spacecraft. Take big, slow steps around the moon. Gather some space rocks; then prepare for your safe return home.

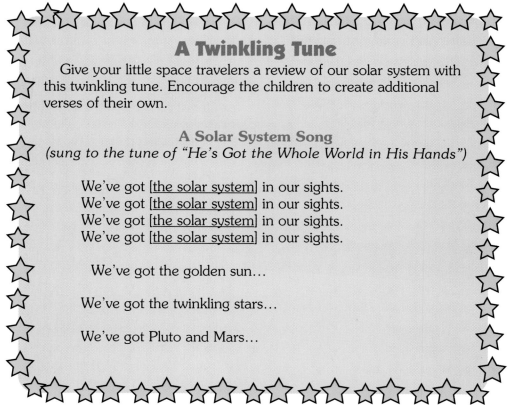

ABC Space

Reinforce the alphabet with this exploration of space vocabulary. To prepare, write the alphabet in a left-hand column of a sheet of chart paper. Then read several books to the class about astronauts and the solar system. Encourage the children to think of space-related words that represent each letter of the alphabet, such as *astronaut, blastoff,* and *constellation.* If desired, accept more than one response for each letter. Add to the list daily as your unit continues. Once the list is complete, encourage each youngster to illustrate one or more words from the list. Label each drawing and highlight the letter of the alphabet it represents. Put the drawings in alphabetical order, and add a cover with the title "ABC Space." Reviews of this class book will be sky-high!

Astronaut Adventure

Launch into circle time with these astronaut antics.

Astronaut, astronaut, turn around.   Turn around.
Astronaut, astronaut, touch the ground.   Touch the ground.
Astronaut, astronaut, leap so high.   Jump.
Astronaut, astronaut, reach the sky.   Stand on toes with arms reaching up.
Astronaut, astronaut, fly around Mars.   Pretend to fly with arms to sides.
Astronaut, astronaut, touch the stars.   Open/close hands like twinkling stars.
Astronaut, astronaut, walk on the moon.   Take big, slow steps.
Astronaut, astronaut, come home soon.   Sit down, pretzel-style.

Space

Space Mobiles

These space mobiles may encourage some imaginary intergalactic adventures! Invite each child in a small group to trace stencils or cookie cutters in a variety of space shapes—such as circles, crescents, and stars—onto construction paper. Have him cut out each shape; then ask him to punch holes in opposite ends of each cutout (as shown). Next, help him thread a paper clip through a hole in one of his cutouts. Instruct him to link a few more paper clips to the first paper clip; then have him connect a second cutout to the end of his paper-clip chain. Direct the child to add each cutout to his space mobile in the same manner. Hang all the mobiles from your ceiling for a moon- and star-spangled scene.

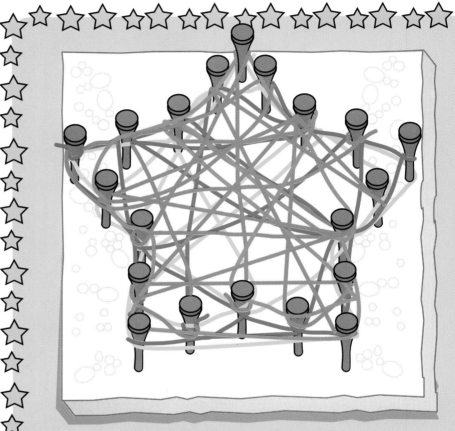

Star-Studded Structure

You bet the stars will be out at this center! To prepare, collect a large Styrofoam® block, golf tees, and several lengths of yarn. Pencil a large star shape on the foam block. Then insert golf tees into the foam along the perimeter of the star shape, making sure you have a tee at each point and corner of the star (as shown). Then knot a loop at each end of each yarn length so that the loop fits over a tee.

To use this center, a child loops one end of a length of yarn over a tee. He then weaves and wraps his yarn around and across the tees to create a design. When the child reaches the end of his yarn, he secures the premade loop over the closest peg. If he desires, he can continue by adding another yarn length to his design. Invite each child to show his star design to the next center visitor; then have the pair cooperatively remove the yarn so that the newcomer can design his own starry delight.

Glimmering Galaxies

Propel youngsters' imaginations into unexplored dimensions of the universe when they design these play dough galaxies. To prepare, add shiny star- and moon-shaped confetti (or regular glitter) to your play dough. Then show students how to roll balls in different sizes to make planets for a solar system. Invite students to add features to their planets. For example, press the end of an unsharpened pencil into a planet to create craters. Or make rings around a planet with play dough ropes. Curve and flatten a short play dough rope to create a crescent moon to orbit a planet. After youngsters' creations are complete, encourage them to share stories about their imaginary travels to these glimmering galaxies.

Stargazing

Your students will be starstruck with this activity! To prepare, set up your art center with star-shaped cookie cutters, sheets of 12" x 18" black construction paper, several trays of different paint colors, and iridescent glitter. Invite each little one to press a cookie cutter into the paint; then have her print star shapes onto a sheet of black construction paper. Before the paint dries, instruct her to sprinkle glitter onto the star outlines. Then have her shake the excess glitter off her paper and set the project aside to dry. Display these dazzling pictures on the ceiling for some spectacular stargazing.

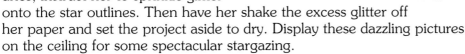

A Lunar Landing

Your little space travelers will get plenty of fine-motor practice while visiting the moon! In advance, collect dress-up items to represent articles that an astronaut might wear, such as an oversized gray sweat suit, heavy work gloves, adult-sized rubber boots, and a bike helmet. Take a photograph of each child dressed in the space gear; then carefully cut around each child's body to remove the background of the picture.

Invite each child to cut the corners of a 12" x 12" yellow construction paper square to create a round moon. Have him punch holes to make craters in his paper moon. (He'll need to fold the paper to punch holes in the center.) Then have him glue his picture to his moon. Encourage him to draw a rocket ship next to his photo. Add a speech bubble with the child's dictation, as shown. This lunar landing is sure to be the journey of a lifetime!

Space

Shooting Stars

These celestial wands are the perfect prop for a star-studded movement exploration. In advance, cut out two tagboard stars and five 12-inch lengths of ribbon for each child. To make a stick for each child's wand, roll a 9" x 12" sheet of construction paper on the diagonal; then hold the paper together with clear tape. Distribute the stars, ribbons, and paper sticks. Have each youngster glue her ribbons to one end of her stick, and glue glitter to one side of each of her stars. Help each child staple her paper stick between the back sides of her two stars. Then add some music, and your little ones will be ready to explore space as they dance and wave their shooting stars.

"Astro-Aerobics"

Astronauts must be in shape to travel in space, so set up your very own astronaut training center at Mission Control (your classroom). Start each morning with a little "astro-aerobic" exercise for your space-flight trainees. Ask youngsters to reach for the sky, bend and touch their toes, jog in place, or run laps around the playground. Then they'll be ready to suit up and take off!

Unidentified Flying Objects

Journey to the outer limits as your astronauts send their own flying saucers into flight. Collect a round plastic lid (such as a coffee can lid) for each child. Distribute the lids; then have each child warm up for this space exploration by circling the saucer (lid) around his waist, head, ankles, legs, etc. Next, have youngsters line up side by side behind a designated baseline. Encourage them to throw their flying saucers as far as they can; then mark each spaceship's landing site with a craft stick. Challenge youngsters to fly their saucers farther each time. It's a bird! It's a plane! No, it's a flying saucer!

Rocket Into Action

Watch enthusiasm take off as your little rocketeers play this circle game. Hold hands in a circle and chant this rockin' rhyme.

Rocket round the sun. Rocket round the moon. | *Circle left.*
Rocket round the stars in the early afternoon. | *Circle right.*
Rocket to the middle. | *Walk to center of circle.*
Rocket up high. | *Wave arms up high.*
Rocket back to outer space. | *Return to outer circle.*
Then fall from the sky! | *Fall to the floor.*

Moon Walk

Send your little space travelers flying high with a walk on the moon. In advance, cut a six-foot-long strip of bulletin board paper, and crumple up a few sheets of gray construction paper to resemble moon rocks. Fill the bottom of a large dishpan with blue fingerpaint. Spread the bulletin board paper on a sidewalk or blacktop area. Set the dishpan at one end of the paper. Then place the moon rocks on the paper, with an approximately equal distance between each one.

Have one child at a time take off his footwear, then step into the paint and onto the strip of paper. Instruct the child to take giant steps over the moon rocks as he walks the length of the paper. While the paint is wet, sprinkle the footprints with stardust (star confetti or glitter). It may be a small step for man, but it's a giant step for "childkind"!

Space

Space Snack

Ingredients:
1 graham cracker per child
chocolate frosting
1 Danish wedding cookie per child
star-shaped decorating sprinkles

Utensils and Supplies:
1 plastic knife (or craft stick) per child
napkins

Teacher Preparation:
Arrange the ingredients and utensils near the step-by-step direction cards.

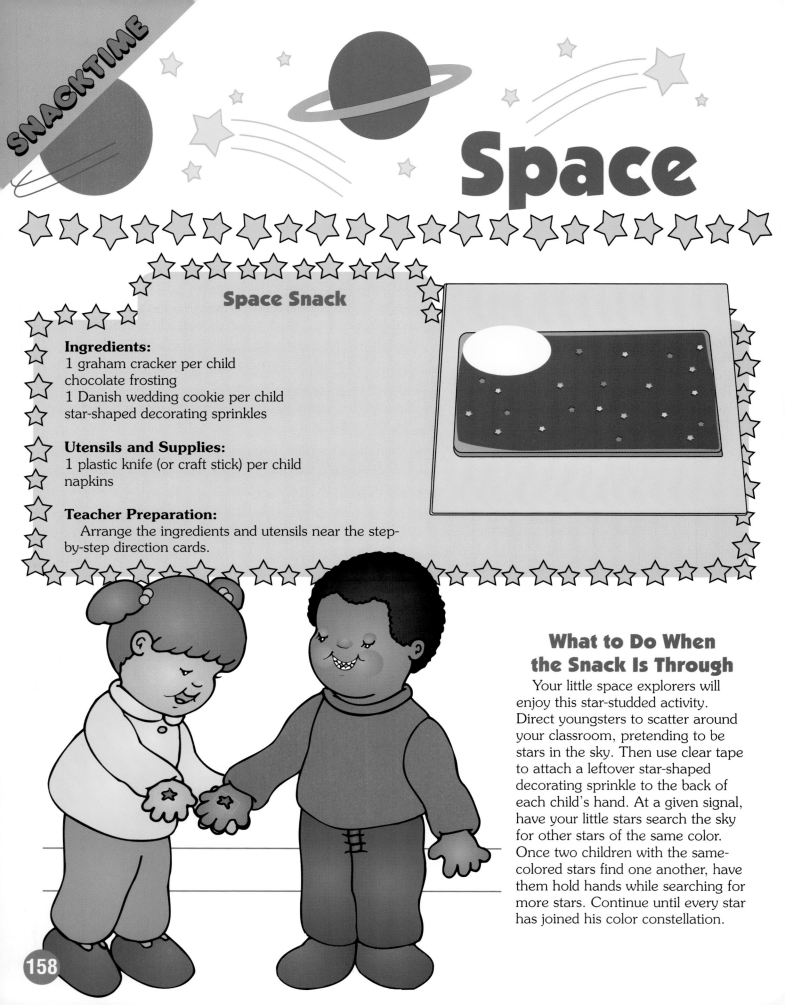

What to Do When the Snack Is Through

Your little space explorers will enjoy this star-studded activity. Direct youngsters to scatter around your classroom, pretending to be stars in the sky. Then use clear tape to attach a leftover star-shaped decorating sprinkle to the back of each child's hand. At a given signal, have your little stars search the sky for other stars of the same color. Once two children with the same-colored stars find one another, have them hold hands while searching for more stars. Continue until every star has joined his color constellation.

3 spread

CHOCOLATE FROSTING

6 out of this world!

2 put

5 put stars

1 wash

Space Snack

4 put moon

Space

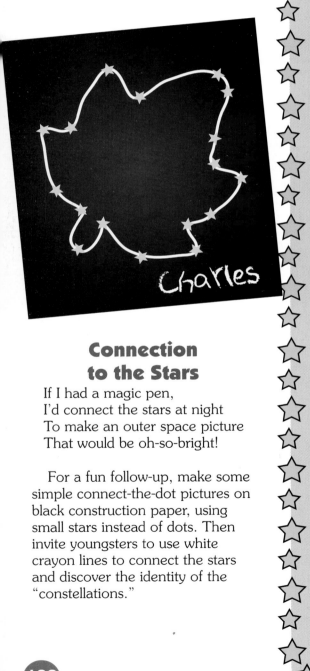

Charles

Connection to the Stars

If I had a magic pen,
I'd connect the stars at night
To make an outer space picture
That would be oh-so-bright!

For a fun follow-up, make some simple connect-the-dot pictures on black construction paper, using small stars instead of dots. Then invite youngsters to use white crayon lines to connect the stars and discover the identity of the "constellations."

Planets Go Round the Sun

Round your youngsters up for a trip around the sun. First write the names of the planets on separate tagboard cards. (If desired, glue a picture of each planet to the corresponding sign.) Then label and draw the sun on another tagboard sign. Attach a length of yarn to each card to create a necklace. Then give each of ten students a sign to wear. Instruct students to hold hands and form a circle. Then have the child representing the sun stand in the center of the circle. As you sing this song, encourage students to slowly circle around the sun. Then, as each planet is named, have the child with the corresponding sign step inside the circle and move around the sun.

(sung to the tune of "Here We Go Round the Mulberry Bush")

Here we go round the powerful sun,
The powerful sun, the powerful sun.
Here we go round the powerful sun,
We are the solar system.

The planet [Mercury] goes round the sun,
Round the sun, round the sun.
The planet [Mercury] goes round the sun,
It's part of the solar system.

Repeat the second verse for each planet, in sequence:

Venus
Earth
Mars
Jupiter
Saturn
Uranus
Neptune
Pluto

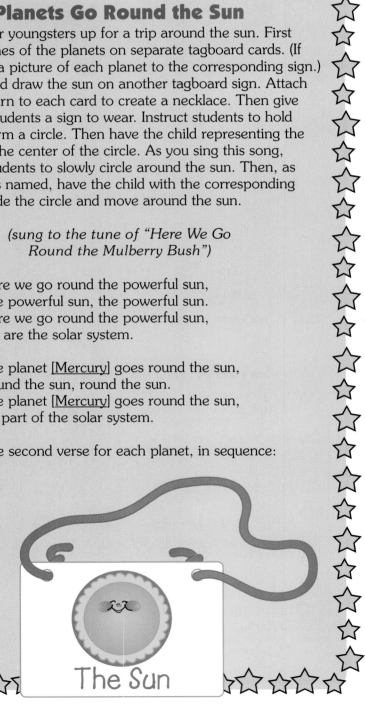

The Sun

Twinkle's Truth

After discussing facts about stars, teach your class this song about the true identity of Twinkle.

(sung to the tune of "Twinkle, Twinkle, Little Star")

Twinkle, twinkle, little star,
Now I know just what you are.
You're a ball of burning gas,
Far away and oh-so-vast.
Twinkle, twinkle, little star,
Now I know just what you are!

Night Sky
(sung to the tune of "Are You Sleeping?")

In the night sky,
In the night sky,
I *see* [stars],
I *see* [stars],
Glowing all around me,
Glowing all around me.
What a sight!
What a night!

Repeat the song, inserting *the moon* and then *planets* for the underlined words. (You might explain that some stars seen at night are actually faraway planets.)

Our Moon, Our Earth

Our moon is made of rock—
Around our earth it runs.

Earth is made of land and sea.
It rotates round the sun.

Hold up right fist.
Rotate right fist around left fist.

Hold up left fist only.
Rotate left fist around opened right hand.

Space

Mooncake

Cook up some fun with a reading of *Mooncake* by Frank Asch (Aladdin Paperbacks). Then follow up with your own recipe for mooncake. In advance, combine in a blender (or with a mixer) one quart of vanilla ice cream and a 12-ounce can of frozen lemonade. Blend the mixture until it is soft; then scoop it into a round cake pan and freeze it. After reading the book aloud to your class, invite them to climb into their rocket ships (under desks or tables) and prepare for a journey to the moon. Begin a countdown, but have them pretend to fall asleep before reaching the number 1, just as Bear did in the story. When they "awaken," they will find themselves on the moon! They're sure to be hungry from their trip, so give each space traveler a plastic spoon and a cup. Invite each child to use an ice-cream scoop to serve herself some mooncake. Mmmmm...out of this world!

Note: This recipe makes enough for 15–20 single scoops.

Zoom! Zoom! Zoom! I'm Off to the Moon!

Read *Zoom! Zoom! Zoom! I'm Off to the Moon!* by Dan Yaccarino (Scholastic Trade Books) and take rhyming to the outer limits! Take advantage of the rollicking rhymes in this story to build language skills. As you read the story aloud a second time, invite the children to complete selected rhymes from the book, such as these:

Zoom! Zoom! Zoom! I'm off to the ___. *(Moon)*
Up, up, and away, I'm leaving ____. *(today)*
There's outer space all over the ____. *(place)*
Floating around without a _____. *(sound)*

Then challenge youngsters further by providing only one rhyming word from the text and asking students to provide the word that rhymes with it, such as *space* and *place*. Watch those rhyming skills rocket sky-high!

Me and My Place in Space

Blast off your unit on space with a reading of *Me and My Place in Space* by Joan Sweeney (Dragonfly Books). After reading the story, discuss how all the planets—including Earth—circle around the sun. To illustrate this concept, have each youngster cut out a yellow construction paper circle and glue it to the center of a sheet of black paper. Then place the black paper inside a box lid. Drop a marble dipped in fluorescent paint inside the lid, and then move the box in a circular motion to make the marble planet rotate around its paper sun. It's "sun-sational!"

I Want to Be an Astronaut

Shoot for the stars with a reading of *I Want to Be an Astronaut* by Byron Barton (HarperCollins Children's Books). After sharing the story, return to the pages that show the astronauts floating in space and explain the term *zero gravity*. Then demonstrate the concept with this gravity game. Ask the children to form a circle around you in an open space. Blow up a balloon and explain that they are all on a team playing against *gravity*—the force that is pulling the balloon down to Earth. The object of the game is to try to keep the balloon up in the air to defeat the force of gravity. If the balloon touches the ground, gravity scores a point. If the team keeps the balloon in the air for a count of three, the team scores a point. May the force be with you!

Grandpa Takes Me to the Moon

After sharing the story *Grandpa Takes Me to the Moon* by Timothy R. Gaffney (William Morrow and Company, Inc.), ignite your youngsters' imaginations by pretending the sand in your sand table is the surface of the moon. Use a spray bottle of water to moisten the sand. Put LEGO® (or DUPLO®) blocks and toy people near the sand table, along with some pebbles, a potato masher, and a small American flag. Have the children use the potato masher to make craters on the moon's surface. Scatter the moon rocks (pebbles). Encourage youngsters to use the blocks to make a moon lander and a lunar rover. Provide Gaffney's book as a reference. Before returning to Earth, have your little astronauts leave their mark by planting the American flag on the moon.

Transportation

Flyin' High, Flyin' Low

Youngsters' understanding of opposites will take flight with these airplanes. To make a simple airplane, help each child glue two wide craft sticks together, as shown. After the glue dries, have him decorate his airplane with markers. Then invite your young pilots to take their airplanes to an open area outdoors for a test flight. Designate yourself as the air traffic controller. Then give youngsters instructions, such as "Fly your plane *high*." Encourage youngsters to "fly" their planes as directed (without really releasing them into the air). Then say, "Fly your plane *low*." Repeat the activity a few times, each time using a different opposite pair, such as *slow/fast* and *straight/crooked*. End your flight with a landing that starts off *rough* and finishes up *smooth*!

Pattern Train

"Choo-choose" this train activity to strengthen patterning skills. In advance, dye a supply of pasta wheels two different colors. To do this, put the pasta into a resealable plastic bag. Add one-half cup of rubbing alcohol and a few drops of food coloring; then shake the bag until the pasta is the desired color. Spread the pasta out on paper towels to dry. Next, cut a supply of rectangles from black construction paper to represent train cars. Place the train cars and pasta wheels in a center.

At this center, a child lines up as many train cars as he desires to make a train. He then adds wheels to his train, creating a color pattern as he works. After he explains his pattern to you or to a classmate, he puts away the wheels and cars for the next pattern engineer to use.

The Transportation Question

Strengthen phonics and language skills with the help of these transportation riddles. To begin, wrap a box and its lid separately in white paper. Write "What am I?" on the box and add several colorful question marks. Place several toy vehicles in the box, such as a car, a bus, a boat, and a plane; then place the lid on the box. During group time, show youngsters the box. Explain that several mystery vehicles are inside the box. Then provide some clues, similar to the ones shown, about one of the mystery items. Challenge youngsters to guess the vehicle by the clues. Confirm correct guesses by removing the vehicle from the box to show to youngsters. To extend this activity, invite youngsters to bring their own transportation toys from home and to make up their own riddles about them.

I have four wheels.
I carry your family from place to place.
I begin with a *c*.
What am I? *(a car)*

I carry many passengers.
I drive on city streets.
I begin with a *b*.
What am I? *(a bus)*

 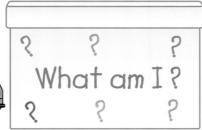

Wheels

Youngsters' counting skills will roll right along with this transportation song. To prepare, duplicate and color the unicycle, bicycle, tricycle, and automobile patterns on page 204. Display the pictures on a flannelboard. Discuss these modes of transportation and ask student volunteers to count the number of wheels on each vehicle before singing this song:

(sung to the tune of "The Wheels on the Bus")

Rollin' down the road on my
  [unicycle],
My [unicycle], my [unicycle].
Rollin' down the road on my
  [unicycle],
I have [one] big wheel(s).

Continue with other verses, substituting the following words and numbers for the underlined words:

bicycle...two
tricycle...three

Highway 123

Take a test drive on Highway 123 to reinforce colors and ordinal numbers. To begin, cut a four-inch-wide length of black bulletin board paper to represent a road. Use chalk to draw the center line on the road; then laminate the paper road for durability. Collect a set of small cars in different colors. Then invite a small student group to drive the cars on the road. After a brief period of exploration, have students line up their cars on the road. Ask the children to name the color of the *first* car. Then ask them to identify the colors of the *second* and *third* cars. Continue in this manner until the ordinal position and color of every car in line has been named. Then have the group repeat the activity using a different color sequence. After several rounds, invite the next group to roll on over for its turn. What a speedy way to learn ordinal numbers!

Transportation

First-Class Flight

If your youngsters have been learning about air travel, this center idea is just the ticket! To begin, arrange chairs to represent the cabin and cockpit of an airplane. Lay a belt on each seat; then put a magazine under each passenger's seat. Provide a tray of plastic cups and play food for flight attendants to serve to the passengers. After the plane is prepared for takeoff, invite each child in a small group to select a role to assume, either as the pilot, a flight attendant, or a passenger. Then have youngsters board the plane. Encourage each child to act out the role he selected. Ladies and gentlemen, welcome aboard!

Here's your drink and pie, ma'am.

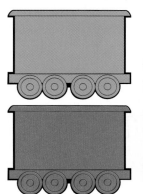

Seriation Station

Invite youngsters to chug on into this sorting-and-seriation station to reinforce color and sequencing skills. First, duplicate ten copies of the train-car pattern on page 205. Color one train car blue, two red, three orange, and four black. Cut out and laminate each pattern; then put them in the math center. Invite your children to sort the train car cutouts by color. Next, have them line up each set of train-car colors to make separate trains. Finally, have students put the color trains in order from shortest to longest. Toot! Toot!

Transportation Mural

Put together sorting skills and art with this transportation mural. To begin, cut a six-foot length each of blue and green bulletin board paper. Tape the lengths of paper together to represent an outdoor background with blue for the sky and green for the ground. Cut out a large lake shape from another piece of blue bulletin board paper. Glue the lake cutout onto the outdoor background. Then cut out pictures of different kinds of vehicles from magazines and travel brochures. Place the background paper and the vehicle cutouts in a center along with glue, paintbrushes, and containers of black and white paint.

Encourage youngsters to visit this center and paint train tracks, roads, and clouds on the paper. After the paint dries, have them glue vehicle cutouts to the appropriate sections of the mural—such as boats on the lake, trains on the tracks, and planes in the sky. This depiction of trains, planes, and automobiles is sure to get two thumbs up!

The Wheels Go Round and Round

Transportation was changed forever when man discovered the wheel. Invite your little ones to make this discovery for themselves in your block center. Provide various types of building toys, such as LEGO® and DUPLO® blocks, but remove any wheels or wheeled pieces from the sets. Encourage youngsters in this center to build cars and trains. When they discover that they can't construct a vehicle that can move across the floor with a push, ask them what's missing. Then provide the wheels you've set aside and let them go ahead with their vehicle building. What *would* we do without wheels?

Transportation Tracks

Little ones will make tracks to the sand table for this activity. To prepare, add enough water to the sand so that it will remain wet for a long period of time. (Have a spray bottle of water on hand to wet the sand as needed.) Then place several toy vehicles with different wheel sizes in the sand table. Invite youngsters to drive the vehicles over the wet sand, leaving tire tracks; then have them park the vehicles near the sand table. Encourage the next group of visitors to match the vehicles to the corresponding tracks in the sand. To erase the tracks, have students smooth the sand with the palms of their hands. Time to start truckin' and trackin' all over again!

Transportation

A Tremendous Train

Little ones will chug on over to this train-making center for some "wheely" fun fine-motor practice! Stock a center with a large supply of 4" x 8" tagboard rectangles (in a variety of colors), several two-inch tagboard circles, black construction paper, a few hole punchers, scissors, crayons, and a supply of brads. To make a train car at this center, a child traces three wheels onto black construction paper and then cuts them out. He uses a hole puncher to punch three holes in one long side of a tagboard rectangle. Then he pokes a brad through the center of a black paper circle and inserts it into one of the holes. He opens the brad to secure it. Then he adds the other two wheels to his car in the same manner. He then uses crayons to add details to his train car. Invite youngsters to make as many train cars as they like. Display the mounting number of train cars on a classroom wall and watch this activity keep on going!

Licenses for Little Ones

Invite each youngster to design his own personalized tricycle or bicycle license plate with this activity. To prepare, cut a half-sheet of tagboard for each child. Show the class a car license plate from your state. Or take youngsters outdoors to look at the license plates on cars in your school parking lot.

To make a license plate, a child colors a piece of tagboard to resemble the background on your state's license plate. He uses letter and numeral stencils to trace onto his plate the letters for his initials, followed by the numeral for his age. Then he traces over each letter and numeral with glue. He sprinkles glitter onto the glue and allows it to dry. Then he punches a hole in each top corner of his license plate and attaches a length of yarn. Invite each child to take his personal license plate home to hang from the handlebars of his trike or bike.

Sink the Boat

Float some scientific discovery into this water-table activity filled with fine-motor opportunities. Put an assortment of toy boats that can be filled with water in your water table. Then add spray bottles, squeeze bottles, turkey basters, funnels, medicine droppers, and measuring cups to the water. Invite small groups of children to the water table for a period of free exploration. Then challenge each child to try to sink a boat into the water. To do this, have her fill a boat with water using the water tool of her choice. After her boat sinks, invite her to empty the boat, then try to sink it again using a different water tool. After several rounds, ask each child to name her tool preference for sinking a boat and the reasons for her choice. Then ask youngsters to explain what made the boats sink. The cause is sure to surface—just "weight" and see!

Just "Plane" Fun

Invite students to fly the friendly skies with their own fun-fold airplanes! Give each child an 8 1/2" x 11" sheet of copy paper and one paper clip. Instruct her to decorate both sides of her paper with crayons. Then show the child how to fold her paper into an airplane following the diagram shown. Then have each child attach her paper clip to the part of the plane that she believes will help it fly best. Line up students on one side of the room. On a signal, invite youngsters to send their planes flying across the room. Have them decide which planes flew the farthest. Invite them to reposition their paper clips, if they desire, to prepare their planes for the next round of takeoffs.

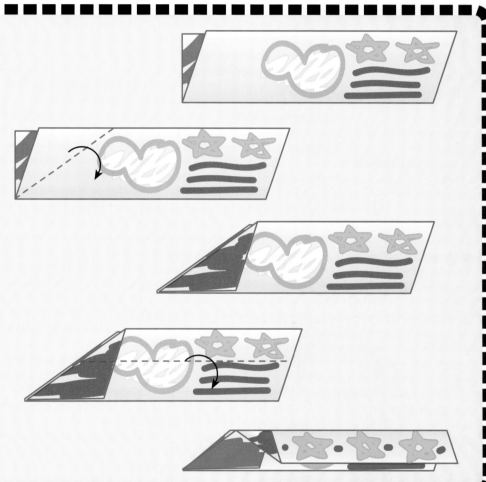

Packing for a Trip

Bring in a suitcase and some old clothes for this activity packed with fine-motor practice. First, set up your dramatic-play area to resemble an airport or train station. Then set up this center nearby. Provide a suitcase, clothing with a variety of fasteners, empty travel bottles, and a zippered cosmetic case or man's shaving kit. Explain to youngsters that if they plan to go on an imaginary trip, they must pack their clothes and toiletries first! Have students at this center zip, button, and snap the clothes before folding them and putting them in the suitcase. Have them screw the tops onto all the travel bottles and then put them in their case before zipping it closed and adding it to the suitcase. Have the children fasten any straps on the inside of the suitcase, then zip or buckle it closed. Ready? Load that luggage on the plane or train and let's go!

Transportation

"Chew-Chew" Train

Ingredients:
1 chocolate-covered cake roll per child
Oreo O's™ cereal

Utensils and Supplies:
3 coffee stirrers per child
napkins

Teacher Preparation:
   Arrange the ingredients and utensils near the step-by-step direction cards.

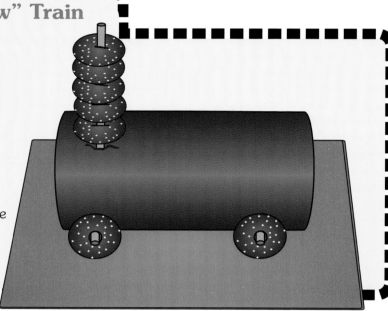

What to Do When the Snack Is Through

   Use the leftover cereal pieces and some more coffee stirrers to give youngsters practice with estimation. Provide each child with a coffee stirrer, a bit of play dough, and a handful of Oreo O's™ cereal. Have him stick his blob of play dough on a tabletop, then push his coffee stirrer into the play dough so that it stands upright. Then ask him to estimate how many cereal pieces will fit on the coffee stirrer. Can he fit ten? More than ten? Have him stack the cereal pieces on his coffee stirrer to find the answer.

"Chew-Chew" Train

wash 1

put 2 2

put 4 3

put 4

push in 5

put 5 6

©The Education Center, Inc. • Busy Kids® Busy Days—Spring & Summer • TEC545

Way to Go

(sung to the tune of "If You're Happy and You Know It")

If the road's the way you go,
Take a car.
If the road's the way you go,
Take a car.
If the road's the way you go,
You can take it fast or slow.
If the road's the way you go,
Take a car.

If the sky's the way you go,
Take a plane.
If the sky's the way you go,
Take a plane.
If the sky's the way you go,
You can take it high or low.
If the sky's the way you go,
Take a plane.

If the sea's the way you go,
Take a boat.
If the sea's the way you go,
Take a boat.
If the sea's the way you go,
You can take it fast or slow.
If the sea's the way you go,
Take a boat.

Who's Driving?

*(sung to the tune of "Do You
Know the Muffin Man?")*

Do you know the bus driver,
The bus driver, the bus driver?
Do you know the bus driver
Who drives the bus through town?

Do you know the airplane pilot,
Airplane pilot, airplane pilot?
Do you know the airplane pilot
Who flies planes in the sky?

Do you know the engineer?
The engineer, the engineer?
Do you know the engineer
Who drives trains on the track?

Do you know the sea captain?
Sea captain, sea captain?
Do you know the sea captain
Who steers the ships at sea?

Travelin' Tune

Use this travelin' tune to review
colors while you reinforce the different modes of transportation. Afterward, invite youngsters to illustrate each verse.

*(sung to the tune of
"Found a Peanut")*

Saw a [red car], saw a [red car],
Saw a [red car] on the [street].
Just now I saw a [red car].
Saw a [red car] on the [street].

Create additional verses about
other forms of transportation by
replacing the underlined words
with these phrases, or create your
own phrases to fit into the song.

Saw a black train…on the track.
Saw a blue plane…in the sky.
Saw a white ship…in the sea.

Driving Signals

Stop little ones in their tracks with this traffic light poem. If desired, make
a tagboard traffic light to use with the poem. To make one, cut out three
circles from a large rectangular piece of tagboard. Back each circle with a
piece from a colored transparent folder (available at office supply stores) so
that the top circle resembles a red light, the center circle a yellow light, and
the bottom circle a green light. Then have your class line up, leaving an
arm's length between each child. Invite students to pretend they are driving
cars as they recite the rhyme. To use the traffic light, shine a flashlight
through each colored light to signal your little drivers during the rhyme.

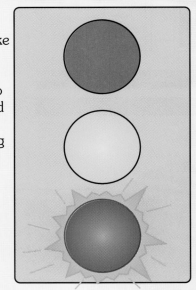

Red light, red light.
No! No! No!   *Stand still and shake head no.*
Yellow light, yellow light.
Slow! Slow! Slow!   *"Drive" slowly.*
Green light, green light.
Go! Go! Go!   *"Drive" carefully.*

173

Transportation

Freight Train

All aboard! Start your transportation unit off on the right track with Donald Crews' *Freight Train* (Mulberry Books). After enjoying this colorful book of chug-along movement, set up your very own train-making station with DUPLO® or LEGO® blocks and varied lengths of colorful yarn. Demonstrate for your little engineers how to use the yarn to connect the blocks together like a train. Lay one end of a length of yarn between two stacked blocks; then snap the blocks together to secure the yarn. Continue to snap pairs of blocks together with the yarn in between until you have your very own train to chug along on the floor. After practicing this train-making technique, encourage youngsters to look in the story for other objects to build with the blocks, such as tunnels and trestles. Full steam ahead!

Wheels on the Bus

Sing merrily along to the familiar text of *Wheels on the Bus,* a Raffi Songs to Read® book (Crown Publishers, Inc.). While this humorous book deals with city transportation, your children may be more familiar with a school bus. So encourage them to sing these additional verses about how to be safe and polite on a school bus.

The wheels on the bus go round and round,
Round and round, round and round.
The wheels on the bus go round and round,
On the way to school.

The children on the bus stay in their seats....
The children on the bus talk quietly....
The children on the bus exit in a line....
The children on the bus thank the bus driver....

Let's Fly From A to Z

Watch skills take off after a reading of Doug Magee and Robert Newman's *Let's Fly From A to Z* (Cobblehill Books). Use this alphabet book about airplanes to reinforce letter skills. For younger students, give each child a die-cut letter and ask him to hold it up when you read about an aircraft item that begins with his letter. For older students, use the book as motivation to create a transportation alphabet book. Write the letters of the alphabet in a column on a sheet of chart paper. Brainstorm together transportation words that begin with each letter. (Encourage the children to refer to classroom transportation books for help.) Once the list is complete, ask youngsters to illustrate the words from your list, making a separate page for each word. Add text to each illustration, such as "A is for airplane." Bind the pages in alphabetical order between construction paper covers and add the title "The ABCs of Transportation." Don't be surprised to find a traffic jam at your reading center!

C is for canoe.

Fire Engines

Anne Rockwell's *Fire Engines* (Puffin Books) describes all the modes of transportation that firefighters use. After sharing the book, teach children the following countdown fingerplay about firefighters and their vehicles. Encourage youngsters to hold up the corresponding number of fingers to represent the firefighters. As you recite the rhyme together, show the pages from the story that feature the named vehicles.

Five firefighters, ready every day.
To the ladder truck! There's a call today!
Four firefighters, ready every day.
To the pumper truck! There's a call today!
Three firefighters, ready every day.
To the ambulance! There's a call today!
Two firefighters, ready every day.
To the fireboat! There's a call today!
One firefighter, ready every day.
He's the chief, and he leads the way!

Boats Afloat

A reading of *Boats Afloat* by Shelley Rotner (Orchard Books) will chart the course for a boat-building center. In advance, ask youngsters to bring to school items that float, such as foam meat trays, milk cartons, margarine tubs, bars of Ivory® soap, sponges, and wood scraps. Set up a center with toothpicks, craft sticks, craft foam, glue, and the items brought from home. Then invite youngsters to create their own unique ship designs using the materials provided. Encourage the children to refer to the book to help them decide which types of boats to build. Provide rocks for barges, netting for fishing boats, toy airplanes and helicopters for aircraft carriers, and toy people for ferries. Once youngsters have completed their ships, have them test the waters at your water table to see if their boats are truly shipshape. Bon voyage!

zebra

ANIMAL MAGNETISM

With zoo animals as the main feature, youngsters are sure to be attracted to this prereading activity. Label each of a supply of sentence strips with a zoo animal name and a corresponding stamp, sticker, or drawing that shows the animal. (Use either capital or lowercase letters, to match your set of magnetic letters.) Laminate the strips for durability; then attach magnetic tape to the back of each strip. Place the sentence strips and magnetic letters in a center with a magnetboard or near a metal filing cabinet.

Invite a child at this center to put a sentence strip on the magnetic surface. Then have her spell out the animal name with the magnetic letters, using the sentence strip as a guide. For older students, you might cut each strip apart to separate the animal picture and name. Then have youngsters match each picture to its name before spelling out the word with the magnetic letters.

WILD OPPOSITES

Here's the tall and short of it—youngsters will roar with delight over this opposites exploration. To begin, write "The zebra is fast, but the hippopotamus is slow" on chart paper. Point out that the characteristics of each animal are opposites. Then ask youngsters to name other animals that fit each description. Label a sticky note with each student response; then affix each one over the appropriate animal—zebra or hippopotamus—to create a new sentence. Read each sentence aloud with the class. Then write a different sentence, this time using other animals and opposite characteristics. For instance, you might write "The elephant is big, but the monkey is little." Once again, ask students to brainstorm other animals to insert into the sentence.

cheetah

The zebra is fast,

but the hippopotamus

is slow.

A ZOO REVIEW

Watch little ones go ape over this zoo counting chant. Write the chant on chart paper. Program each of ten sticky notes with a different numeral from 1 to 10. Then teach youngsters the chant. After a few rounds, give each sticky note to a different volunteer. Repeat the chant, inviting each child to affix her sticky note to the matching number word on the chart.

As a variation, print the chant with numerals in place of the number words. Label sticky notes with the corresponding number words for students to match to the chart.

(chanted to the tune of "One, Two, Buckle My Shoe")

One, two, who's at the zoo?
Three, four, lions galore.
Five, six, birds and fish.
Seven, eight, bears and apes.
Nine, ten, the fun never ends!

> 1 , 2 , who's at the zoo?
>
> 3 , four, lions galore.
>
> Five, six, birds and fish.
>
> Seven, eight, bears and apes.
>
> Nine, ten, the fun never ends!

THIS PLACE IS A ZOO!

Your classroom is bound to look like a zoo when youngsters bring in toy animals from home for show-and-tell. Invite each child to bring a stuffed zoo animal to share with the class during group time. Then collect all the animals and have students work together to sort the animals into designated categories, such as animal types, colors, or sizes. Use the same categories for some patterning practice with the zoo animals. Ask youngsters to pattern the animals by color (such as brown bear, black gorilla, brown monkey, black panther) or by size (such as giraffe, turtle, ostrich, mouse). Or have youngsters pattern the animals by other characteristics, such as leg count, tail/no tail, or stripes/spots. No matter what pattern you follow, youngsters will have a roaring good time!

COUNT ON ZOO ANIMALS

Assign each little zookeeper to count the animals in his own stamp-art zoo. To prepare, stamp a different zoo animal stamp on each of ten notecards. Then write a numeral from 1 to 10 on each card. Laminate the cards for durability. Then, for each child, fold a large sheet of construction paper twice to create four sections. Place the cards, the unfolded papers, the stamp pads, and the animal stamps in a center.

At this center, a child selects a card and finds the matching animal stamp. Then, on one section of his paper, he stamps the number of animals corresponding to the numeral on the card. He repeats the procedure for each section of his paper. Then he counts the total number of zoo animals on his paper and writes the sum on the back.

FEEDING TIME

Invite youngsters to help the zookeeper feed the animals with this math-center activity. Prepare a simple bar graph by dividing a sheet of chart paper into five columns. Label each column with the name and picture of a different zoo animal. Make 15 construction paper copies of the bucket pattern on page 205; then cut out and laminate the patterns. Tape-record yourself—the zookeeper—giving feeding instructions for each animal on the graph. For example, you might say, "Give the zebra one bucket of food" or "Give the elephant four buckets of food." Leave a long pause after each direction. Then record questions such as "Which animal has the most (or fewest) buckets of food?" and "How many more buckets of food does the [elephant] have than the [zebra]?"

Display the bar graph in your math center. Place the tape in a tape recorder, and arrange it, along with the feeding buckets and a supply of Sticky-Tac, in the center. Invite each child who visits this center to listen to the tape and attach the buckets to the graph as directed. Encourage youngsters to answer the questions at the end of the tape.

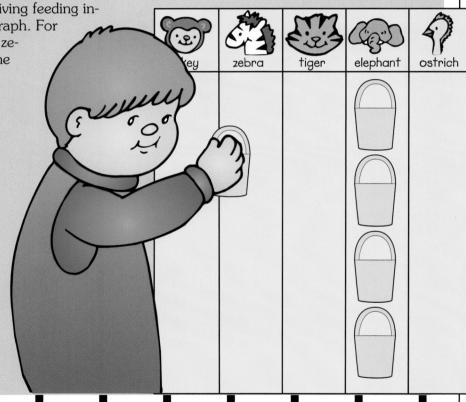

WHO BELONGS IN THE ZOO?

Which animals belong in the zoo? Use this block-center idea to see if your youngsters know. Place an assortment of toy animals in your block center, including zoo animals, farm animals, ocean animals, and house pets. Invite students to build zoo habitats with the blocks, adding rocks, green Easter grass, and plastic trees if they desire. Then ask students to separate the zoo animals from the other animals and place them in their new zoo homes. After they settle the zoo animals in, invite your little ones to line up the remaining animals for a tour of the zoo.

"PUZ-ZOO-ZLES"

Have youngsters practice sorting and sequencing skills as they assemble these puzzling zoo animals. Cut several large pictures of different zoo animals from nature magazines. Mount the pictures onto tagboard cards; then laminate the cards for durability. Cut each card into three vertical sections to create a simple animal puzzle. Then put all the puzzle pieces in a container.

To use this center, a child first sorts the pieces according to the puzzle to which they belong, then puts the strips in order to complete each animal "puz-zoo-zle."

SPOTS AND STRIPES

This activity will have your little artists spotting zoo animals of all kinds at your art center. Hang several pictures of spotted and striped zoo animals—such as zebras, tigers, giraffes, and leopards—in your art center. Set out zoo-animal stencils, markers, trays of paint, some round corks, and a few plastic hair combs.

Invite each youngster at this center to draw or trace a zoo animal. Have her dip a cork in paint to make spots on her animal. Or have her comb paint over her animal outline to give it stripes. After the paint dries, display these animals in a prominent place for all to spot!

GOIN' WILD

Youngsters will be wild about this dramatic-play center activity. To prepare, ask parents to donate old Halloween costumes of zoo animals (or items that can be used to create animal costumes) and pairs of old gloves. Hot-glue construction paper claws to the gloves. If desired, make animal-ear headbands from sentence strips. Place the costume items in your dramatic-play center. Then invite visitors to this center to assemble their own zoo-animal costumes for some role-playing fun. Students will have a roaring good time!

water   land

ZOO HABITATS

Here's a tune about animal habitats that really hits home. To prepare, gather pictures of various animals that live in the water and on land. Label the top of a piece of chart paper with the headings "Water" and "Land." Add a small drawing of waves and a sketch of grass and a tree to cue nonreaders.

Show youngsters the animal pictures and discuss where each animal lives. As you sing the following song, hold up each animal picture. Then solicit your students' help in taping the animal picture under the corresponding habitat.

OH WHERE, OH WHERE?
(sung to the tune of "Oh Where, Oh Where Has My Little Dog Gone?")

Oh where, oh where does a [dolphin] live?
Oh where, oh where is his home?
Does he live in water or on the land?
Oh where, oh where does he roam?

FEEDING TIME

Ready for feeding-time frenzy at the zoo? Talk about the different kinds of foods zoo animals eat; then sing this song. If desired, follow up with a related reading of *Sam Who Never Forgets* by Eve Rice (Greenwillow Books).

(sung to the tune of "Ten Little Indians")

One little, two little, three little fishies,
Four little, five little, six little fishies,
Seven little, eight little, nine little fishies,
To feed the hungry seals.

One pail, two pails, three pails of oats,
Four pails, five pails, six pails of oats,
Seven pails, eight pails, nine pails of oats,
To feed the hungry zebras.

One ripe, two ripe, three ripe bananas,
Four ripe, five ripe, six ripe bananas,
Seven ripe, eight ripe, nine ripe bananas,
To feed the hungry monkeys.

ANONYMOUS ANIMALS

Take your students on an imaginary walk through the zoo! Ask your little ones to pretend that they have just arrived at the zoo. Ask them to close their eyes and try to picture what it looks like. Verbally walk them through the main gate as you describe the sounds, smells, and sights. At the first animal exhibit, give the children a series of clues to help them guess the identity of the animal. For example, your clues might include: "This animal has four legs. It has orange and black stripes." When your students have arrived at a guess, encourage them to make the sound of the mystery animal (for example a loud tiger roar). Continue your walk through the zoo, describing more animals that you meet along the way.

ZOO GROUPS

This sorting activity is in a category all its own. Use the animal pictures gathered for "Zoo Habitats" (page 180). Give each child a picture; then call out a feature that some of the animals possess, such as stripes, spots, or tails. If a child is holding an animal that fits the description, have him stand and show his picture. Solicit other attributes by which the animals might be sorted, such as size, number of legs, or habitat.

COUNTING CRITTERS

Count your way through the zoo with this fingerplay adaptation of *Brown Bear, Brown Bear, What Do You See?* by Bill Martin, Jr. (Henry Holt and Company, Inc.).

One bear, one bear, who's with you?	*Wiggle pointer finger.*
Two funny monkeys in the zoo.	*Wiggle two fingers.*
Monkeys, monkeys, who's with you?	
Three striped zebras in the zoo.	*Wiggle three fingers.*
Zebras, zebras, who's with you?	
Four king lions in the zoo.	*Wiggle four fingers.*
Lions, lions, who's with you?	
Five huge elephants in the zoo.	*Wiggle five fingers.*
Elephants, elephants, who's with you?	
Visiting children—just like you!	*Wiggle fingers on both hands.*

MONKEYS WITH THE MUNCHIES

Your youngsters are sure to go ape over making these zoo monkeys with the munchies. To prepare, draw an outline of a tree on a sheet of paper; then make a white construction paper copy for each child. Ask each child to color his tree. Then encourage him to add some monkeys to his tree. Have him press a thumb onto a brown stamp pad (or into brown paint), then press it on his paper. Then have him add a pinky-print head to the thumbprint body. When the ink (or paint) is dry, invite the child to use markers to draw facial features, ears, arms, legs, and tails on his monkeys. As a final touch, have him draw some bananas on his tree. Then give each child a copy of this rhyme. Ask him to fill in the numeral corresponding to the number of monkeys in his tree; then have him attach his poem to his illustration to take home and share with his family.

_____ little monkeys up in a tree,
Looking right down at you and me.
"What do you want, you silly monkeys?"
"We want bananas 'cause we're hungry!"

For added fun, recite this rhyme at snacktime, filling in the number of students in your class in the first line. Invite your little monkeys to recite the last line; then give each of them a banana to peel and eat!

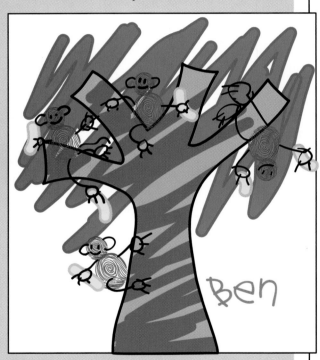

ZANY ZOO ANIMALS

These zany zoo animals stand alone as a fun fine-motor workout. In advance, make one copy of the animal patterns on page 206. Mask each animal's legs; then copy a supply of the animal-body patterns onto tagboard.

Working with one small group at a time, display real photos of the animals shown on the reproducible. Then invite each child to create one of these zoo animals. To make one, cut out an animal pattern. Refer to the picture of the corresponding animal to color both sides of the cutout. Color a pair of clothespin legs; then attach them to the animal. Encourage youngsters to use their stand-up zoo animals in your block center. For some zany zoo fun, invite students to exchange animal legs with one another to create silly animals with mixed-up legs.

FANCY FELINES

These feline creations are "purr-fect" for sharpening fine-motor skills in the play dough area! In advance, enlarge the cat pattern on page 206; then make several tagboard copies. Cut out and laminate the patterns. Place the cutouts in your play dough area along with rolling pins, garlic presses, and scissors. Show your class pictures of different kinds of cats that might be found in a zoo, such as a tiger, a leopard, and a lion. Point out the characteristics of each cat's fur, such as its stripes, spots, or mane. Then invite each child to transform a cat cutout into a fancy zoo cat by adding play dough features to its body. For instance, she might cut play dough ropes to serve as a tiger's stripes. Or she might put small play dough dots on her cat to make a spotted leopard. Or, to create a lion, the child might make a mane from garlic-pressed play dough. You'll hear roars of delight as youngsters make these fancy felines!

WRAPAROUND SNAKES

Wrap up your zoo unit with these wraparound snakes. Gather a class supply of clear straws and pipe cleaners. Instruct each child to cut a straw into 10 to 12 short pieces. Have her bend one end of a pipe cleaner into a loop; then have her thread the straw pieces onto the other end of her pipe cleaner. After she threads all of her straw pieces onto her pipe cleaner, have her loop the straight end to secure the straws. If desired, invite the child to glue small wiggle eyes to one end of her snake. Or have her add spots to the snake's body with a permanent marker. Instruct each child to wrap her snake around a pencil, then gently remove the pencil. Keep an eye on these snakes—they just might slither away!

ZOO SHADOWS

There's not a shadow of a doubt that your children will enjoy tracing these zoo animals. To prepare, duplicate the animal patterns on page 206 and then cut them out. Position an overhead projector so that it faces a bare wall. Provide tape and large sheets of white paper. Invite each child, in turn, to place her choice of animal cutouts on the overhead projector. Then help her tape a sheet of paper to the wall so that it captures the projected shadow of the cutout. Ask the child to trace the shadow of the animal onto her paper. Then have her take her tracing to the easel to paint the animal's features. Encourage her to paint her animal in realistic colors and patterns so that it resembles the real zoo animal. (If desired, display pictures of zoo animals for reference.) After the paint dries, help the child cut out her animal; then group all of the same animals together. Staple each animal group onto a separate section of a bulletin board. Attach black crepe-paper borders around each animal group to create zoo enclosures. Then title this display "A Zoo Review."

ZOO FOOD

Ingredients:
1 flat-bottomed ice-cream cone per child
dried banana chips
Craisins® dried cranberries
Goldfish® crackers
sunflower seeds

Utensils and Supplies:
4 large spoons
knife

Teacher Preparation:
Cut the dried banana chips into smaller pieces. Arrange the ingredients and utensils near the step-by-step direction cards.

WHAT TO DO WHEN THE SNACK IS THROUGH

What sort of fun can you have with leftover zoo food? Sorting fun! Pour any extra banana chips, Craisins® dried cranberries, Goldfish® crackers, and sunflower seeds into one large bowl. Invite each child to spoon some of the mixture onto a napkin. Ask him to group all the same foods together. Ask questions to help youngsters compare the number of items in each group, using words such as *most, fewest,* and *equal.*

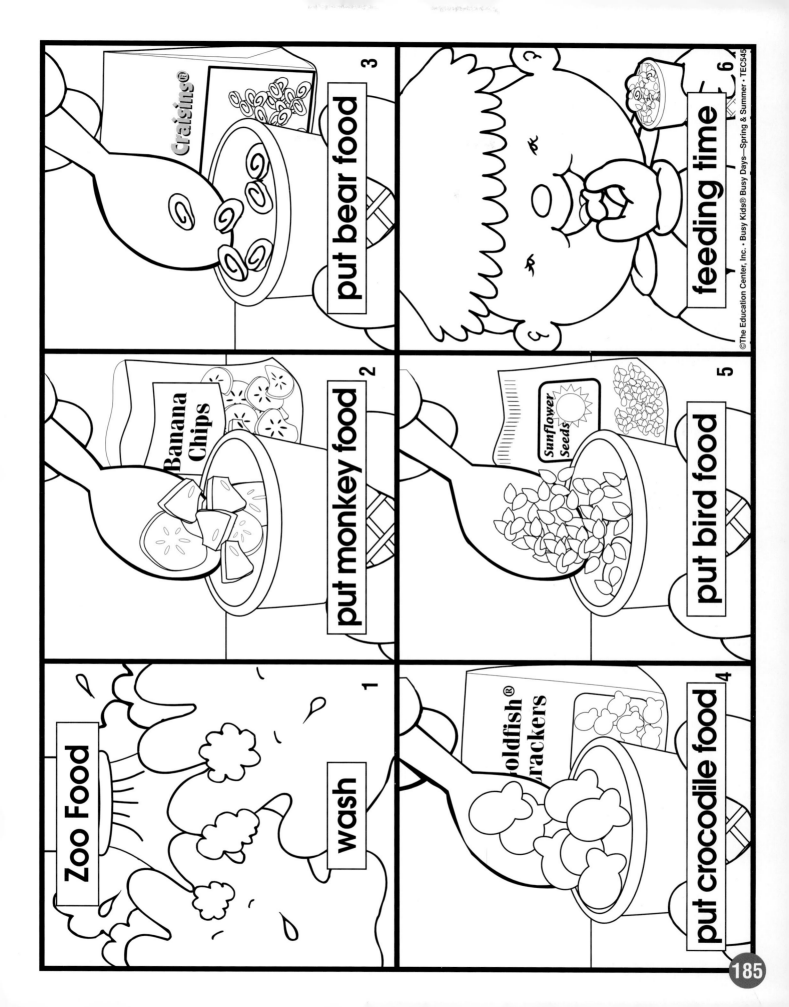

Zoo Food

wash

1

Banana
Chips

put monkey food

2

Craisins®

put bear food

3

Goldfish®
Crackers

put crocodile food

4

Sunflower
Seeds

put bird food

5

feeding time

6

ZOO

MONKEY MIMES

Monkey around the classroom with this rhythm-and-mime rhyme. To begin, share the poem with your class. Then encourage students to imitate your monkey movements as you scratch your head, swing your arms, eat a banana, and mime other monkey-related actions.

Monkey see,
Monkey do.
I'm a monkey
In the zoo.

Monkey see,
Monkey do.
I can [jump up and down].
Can you [jump up and down], too?

A DAY AT THE ZOO

Let's go to the zoo
Early in the day.
We can see the lions eat
And hear what the peacocks say.

Let's go to the zoo
In the afternoon.
We can see the hippo bathe
And hear a dolphin's tune.

Let's go to the zoo
When the sun has set.
We can see the zebra sleep
And hear an owl duet.

THE KEEPER AT THE ZOO

Feed your zoo crew a tune and a snack with this tasty activity. In advance, purchase Craisins®, banana chips, fish-shaped crackers, and sunflower seeds. Mix up a class-sized batch of these snacks to create a zoo snack mix. Then give each child a serving of the mixture on a napkin. Sing the song with your class, pausing after each verse to allow youngsters to taste a tidbit of the featured animal's food. When the song is complete, invite students to munch the rest of their goodies. Yum! Yum!

(sung to the tune of "The Farmer in the Dell")

The keeper at the zoo,
The keeper at the zoo,
Heigh ho! The derry-o!
The keeper at the zoo.

The keeper feeds the [bears].
The keeper feeds the [bears].
Heigh ho! The derry-o!
The keeper feeds the [bears].   *Eat a Craisin®.*

Continue with the following:

The keeper feeds the monkeys....   *Eat a banana chip.*
The keeper feeds the 'gators....   *Eat a fish-shaped cracker.*
The keeper feeds the birds....   *Eat a sunflower seed.*

GUESS THE ZOO ANIMAL

Use this song for a fun zoo guessing game and a preview of a zoo field trip. Sing the verse; then give a clue about a zoo animal, such as "This animal has stripes" or "This animal has a long neck." Challenge youngsters to guess which animal you're thinking of. Then sing the song again and give a new clue about another animal. Once youngsters get the idea, invite one of them to make up clues about the zoo animal of her choice.

(sung to the tune of "This Old Man")

At the zoo,
At the zoo,
Guess what we'll see at the zoo!
I'm thinking of an animal and here's a clue.
Guess what we'll see at the zoo!

ZOO

Charles would like to have a sleepover with a monkey.

GOOD NIGHT, GORILLA

Good Night, Gorilla by Peggy Rathmann (The Putnam Publishing Group) is sure to get your group gigglin' as they watch Gorilla and his friends follow the zookeeper home for an uninvited sleepover! Keep the giggles going with this fun extension. To prepare, duplicate several copies of the small animal patterns on page 207; then cut them apart. Gather the following items for each child: an individual-serving-size cereal box, a 6" x 9" piece of construction paper, a 4" x 4" square of fabric, a school photo, and a 9" x 12" sheet of construction paper.

To make a miniature bed, a child wraps his cereal box in the 6" x 9" construction paper, securing the paper with tape. Next, he chooses a zoo animal cutout and trims around the animal's head. He also trims around his head in his school photo. Then he glues them next to each other as shown. He glues a fabric square to the box to resemble a bed cover. Then he glues the bed to the 9" x 12" sheet of construction paper. Help each child finish his project by programming his sheet similarly to the one shown. Display these bedtime scenes on a bulletin board with the title "Good Night, Zoo!"

ZOO-LOOKING

Enjoy a trip to the zoo as you read *Zoo-Looking* by Mem Fox (Mondo Publishing). After a first reading, share the story again and encourage youngsters to join you as you read the repetitive text. Next, invite your little ones to go "zoo-looking" right in their classroom. To prepare for this activity, enlarge the large animal patterns on page 207 and duplicate them onto tagboard. Color them, and then cut around each animal's head. Tape a craft stick to each one. Give the resulting animal masks to selected youngsters and ask them to stand in different areas of your classroom. Invite other children to take turns role-playing zoo visitors. As a child walks by each animal, ask the class to recite this line from the book: "[Child's name] looked at the [animal's name] and the [animal's name] looked back." Encourage each child holding a mask to make movements or sounds that represent his animal. Continue until every youngster has had a turn to role-play a zoo animal or a zoo visitor.

Rabbit Pattern

Use with *Rabbit's Good News* on page 18.

Shoes Pattern

Use with *The Country Bunny and the Little Gold Shoes* on page 19.

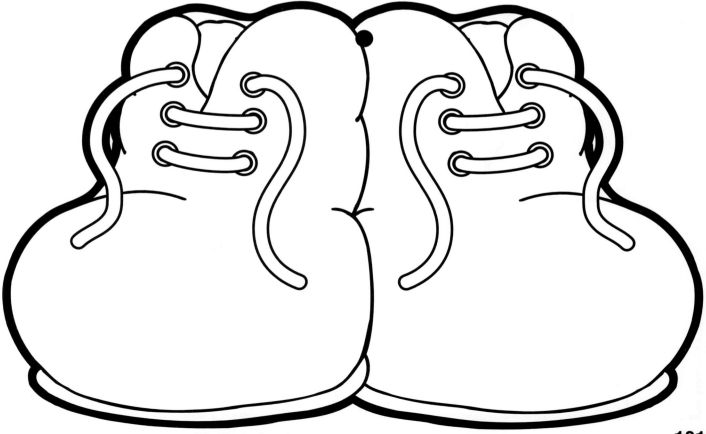

Dinosaur Patterns

Use with "Directional Dinos" on page 40 and "Dinosaur, Dinosaur" and "A Daily Dose of Dinosaur Math" on page 41.

Dinosaur Pattern
Use with "Designer Dinosaurs" on page 42 and
" 'Color-a-saurus' " and "Dino 'Trace-O' " on page 43.

Umbrella Pattern
Use with "Unique Umbrellas" on page 58.

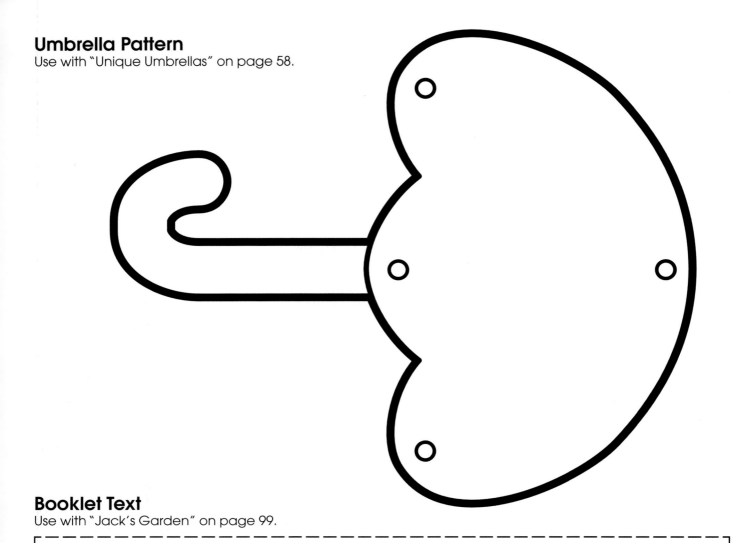

Booklet Text
Use with "Jack's Garden" on page 99.

1. This is the g arden our class planted.

2. This is the soil tha t made up the g arden our class planted.

3. These ar e the seeds tha t we planted in the soil tha t made up the g arden our class planted.

4. This is the rain tha t water ed the seeds tha t we planted in the soil tha t made up the g arden our class planted.

5. And these ar e the plants tha t gr ew after the rain tha t water ed the seeds tha t we planted in the soil tha t made up the g arden our class planted.

Chicken Pattern
Use with "Pickin' 'n'
Peckin'" on page 75.

©The Education Center, Inc.

Vegetable Patterns

Use with "Farmer in the Garden," and "Mystery Veggie" on page 88 and "Read All About It!" on page 89.

198

Dalmatian Pattern
Use with "A Hot Spot for Safety" on page 107.

Sheep Pattern
Use with "Mary's Colorful Lambs," "Hide-and-Sheep," and "Have You Any Wool?" on page 117.

Sea Animal Pictures

Use with "Colorful Sea Creatures" on page 132.

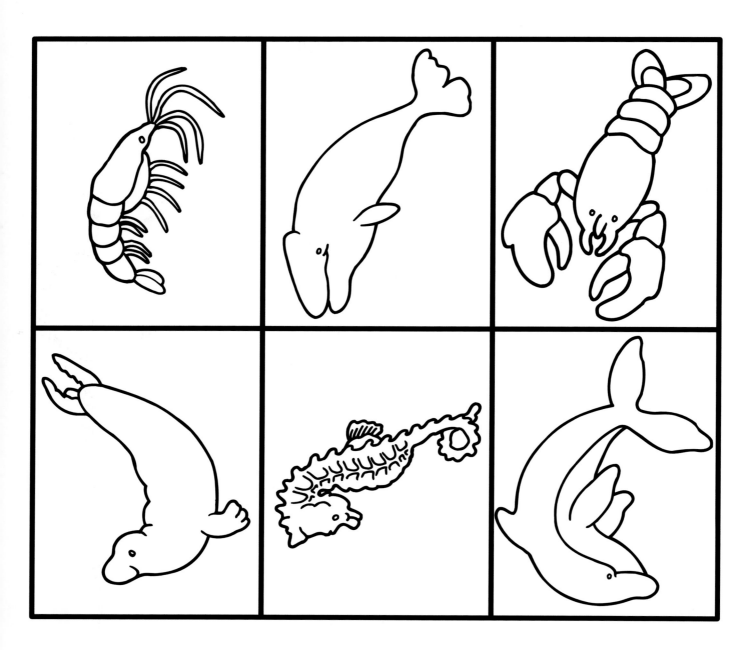

Sand-Pail and Fish Patterns

Use the sand-pail pattern with "Collecting Seashells" on page 134.
Use the fish pattern with "Oceans of Bubbles" on page 135.

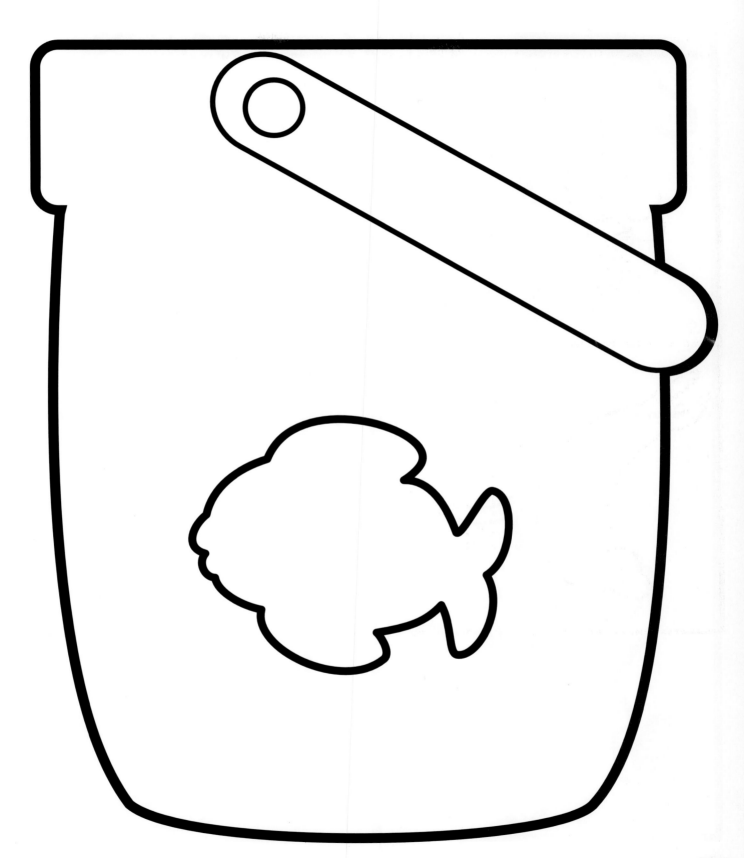

Vehicle Patterns
Use with "Wheels" on page 165.

unicycle

bicycle

tricycle

automobile

Train-Car Pattern

Use with "Seriation Station" on page 166.

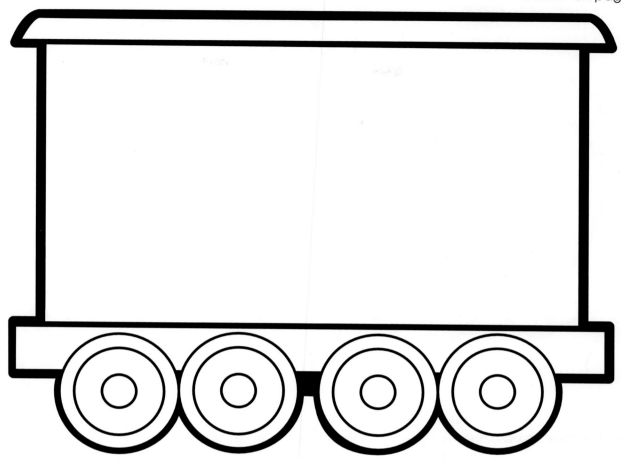

Bucket Pattern

Use with "Feeding Time" on page 178.

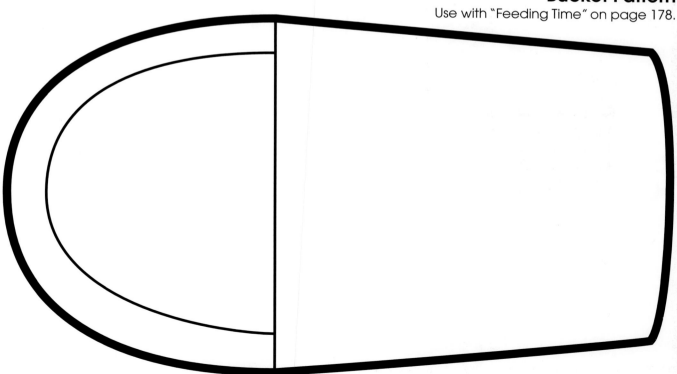

Zoo Animals

Use the cat pattern with "Fancy Felines" on page 183. Use all the patterns with "Zany Zoo Animals" on page 182 and "Zoo Shadows" on page 183.